THE SUPER TEAMS BOOK

For a complete list of Global Management titles,
visit our website at www.goglobalmgt.com or email us at
infoGME@aol.com

THE
SUPER TEAMS
BOOK

Mike Pegg

Published in 2011 by Global Management Enterprises, LLC.
Massachusetts, USA

ISBN 978-161110-023-5

Contents

INTRODUCTION

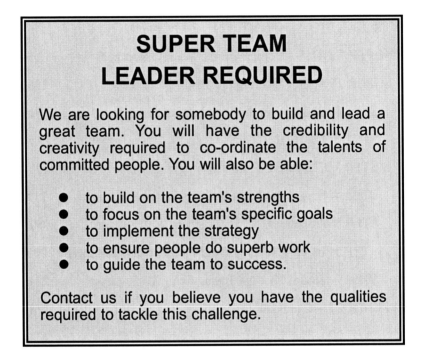

SUPER TEAM LEADER REQUIRED

We are looking for somebody to build and lead a great team. You will have the credibility and creativity required to co-ordinate the talents of committed people. You will also be able:

- to build on the team's strengths
- to focus on the team's specific goals
- to implement the strategy
- to ensure people do superb work
- to guide the team to success.

Contact us if you believe you have the qualities required to tackle this challenge.

Would you be attracted by such an advertisement? If so, how would you apply for the role? How would you convince the potential sponsors? If you got the role, how would you build a peak performing team? How would you achieve the agreed picture of perfection?

'Start by setting up the team to succeed,' advises Paul, a veteran of many turnarounds. 'Enthusiasm is vital, but look before you leap. Painful experiences taught me some hard lessons, so nowadays I do extensive research before taking over a team. Feeling flattered by being approached, I often took management jobs, only to find unmotivated staff or confused goals.

'Before taking a role, get **all** the information. **First, clarify what mountain you are climbing.** Make sure you identify the key sponsors and their picture of success. **Second, clarify the resources required to reach the summit.** Make sure you will have the right backup. **Third, clarify the chances of success.** Make sure it is at least 7/10; otherwise forget it.

'Bearing these findings in mind, decide whether or not you want to embark on the expedition.'

Imagine you took the leadership role: how would you build the team? How would you guide it to success? Try tackling the exercise called *Super Teams* overleaf. Think of a brilliant team in any field. Perhaps it was one you participated in or one you admired from afar. Describe what they did right to perform superbly. How can you follow these paths in your own way? There are many ways to climb a mountain. Similarly, there are many ways to orchestrate people's talents. *The Super Teams Book* explores one approach (see illustration on page 9). Providing you have put the right foundation in place, you can then go through the following steps.

● SPIRIT

Get the right people with the right spirit. Great teams are built on 'Similarity of Spirit and Diversity of Strengths.' (Diversity of spirit is a recipe for disaster.) What qualities will you look for in team members? 'I want people who are positive, professional and, in their own areas, peak performers,' explained one leader. Get the right balance between 'Soul Players' and 'Star Players.' Soul Players embody the spirit of the team. They are consistent players who do the right things day after day. Star Players also embody the spirit, but also add that 'little bit extra.' (There is no place for 'Semi-Detached' Players.) Super Teams are made up of people who behave like volunteers, not victims. Recruit for spirit; then focus on the next step.

SUPER TEAMS

1) Write the name of a Super Team. It can be one you have participated in or one you have admired. It can be from any field, for example, business, sport, the arts or wherever.

● _____

2) Describe what you believe people did right to build the Super Team.

● They _____

● They _____

● They _____

● They _____

● They _____

3) Describe how you can follow these principles in your own way to build your team into a Super Team.

● I can _____

● I can_____

● I can _____

SUPER TEAMS

Start by making clear contracts with your sponsors on the agreed picture of success. You can then focus on the following steps.

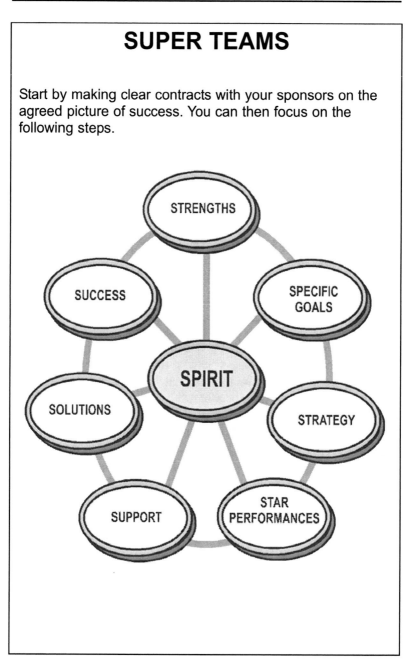

● STRENGTHS

Get people to do what they do best. Positive Modeling is the greatest strength – so start by building a leadership team that will act as good models. Great leaders recognize that they are always 'on stage,' so they must practice what they preach.

Leaders, like parents, create the climate. They must live the message, otherwise it gets diluted. Build on your own strengths as a leader, but surround yourself with complementary skills. Get people who fill the roles of Energizer, Environmentalist and Executor. Looking across the entire team, identify each person's strengths. Ask yourself: "If these people left tomorrow and offered their services back as freelancers, would I hire them? If so, what would I specifically hire them to deliver? Where do they consistently produce As, rather than Bs or Cs?" Compile the team's Strengths Inventory, identify the gaps and get these filled. Then focus on achieving the vision.

● SPECIFIC GOALS

Great leaders inspire people by creating a compelling Picture of Perfection. Acting as Compass Setters, they ensure that everybody knows the 'What.' But, how to make this happen? Starting from the sponsor's goals, clarify the specific results to be achieved. People are more likely to opt-in, however, if they see the benefits. "Human beings will tackle almost any challenge,' it is said, 'providing they understand the 'Why.' " Communicate the pluses involved in achieving the goals, but don't be afraid to outline the minuses. You need 'volunteers' who are prepared to accept both the rewards and risks. The changing world of work has produced a new psychological contract. It is one where:

a) the employer's role is to show people the picture of success
b) the employees' role is to show how they want to contribute to achieving the picture of success
c) they then make clear contracts and work together to achieve the picture of success.

Leaders can provide a compelling vision, but they cannot achieve it alone. Commitment is vital. Bearing in mind the pluses and minuses involved, invite people to decide whether they want to tackle the challenge. Those who opt-in will then give their best to the team.

● STRATEGY

How can you climb the mountain? The vision is the 'What'; the strategies are the 'How.' Clarify the key strategies the team can follow to give itself the greatest chance of success. Bearing these principles in mind, make clear contracts with your people. Clarify: "Who will do What and by When?" Combining everybody's talents will provide the creative edge. Ask yourself: "How can we co-ordinate our strengths to achieve the specific goals?" You may want to adopt an approach called The Best Way. Four rules apply.

1) Get people to do what they do best.
2) Get people to work with colleagues with whom they work best.
3) Get the remaining tasks completed in the way that is best.
4) Get people to make crystal clear contracts about their best contribution to the business. Then it is time to get on with the job.

● STAR PERFORMANCES

Great work comes next. Keep people's eyes on the picture of perfection, but also play to your own strengths. Leaders often follow the STAGE Model. They recognize that the Strategic, Tactical, Administrative, Grunt Work and Emotional parts of the job must be done. Some focus their own efforts on the Strategic and Emotional aspects and, if appropriate, hire a Co-ordinator to orchestrate peoples' talents. Super Teams are highly disciplined and deliver their equivalent of 'The Perfect 10' in Olympic gymnastics. Encourage people to get some early successes, proactively satisfy their sponsors and keep improving their Professional Standards. Stay ahead of the game by ensuring the team still has the right Product, People, Principles, Practice and Performance. Do whatever is necessary to ensure that the teams deliver brilliant work.

● SUPPORT

Encouragement, Enterprise and Excellence are the keys to creating a stimulating environment. Start with the basics. Provide people with the practical and psychological support required to do the job. Pay special attention to the Soul Players. They are often taken for granted, and this can slip over into neglect. Star Players require a different kind of attention. Build on their strengths, but also ensure they take responsibility for contributing towards the team's specific goals. Recognize that 'results require proper rest and recovery.' Encourage people to take time out to relax, re-center and refocus. The business will benefit, because they are then more likely to make good quality decisions and produce better results.

Great teams are resilient, but how to respond when people experience setbacks? Recognize how you can help them go through the Reactive Change Curve. People will emerge tougher, stronger and wiser. Sustain a creative culture. Shine a light on positive actions, but take tough decisions about unacceptable behavior. Never walk past a quality problem. Spend time with your own Encouragers. Why? If your cup runneth over, you will have extra energy to pass on to the team.

• SOLUTIONS

Good navigators chart the route to success, but they also anticipate possible problems. Educate your team to explore any potential 'Sticky Moments.' There are two reasons for taking this step. First, they will find ways to prevent such difficulties occurring or, if necessary, develop solutions. Second, they will expand the team's 'Collective Radar,' increasing their ability to make decisions without looking to you for guidance. You will then be released to shape tomorrow's business, rather than get bogged down in managing today's business. Educate people to also deal with potential success. This is necessary because, after getting early wins, some teams 'Declare victory too early.' Suddenly they lose momentum and slide back down to the bottom of the hill. People must know how to behave in the Green, Amber and Red Zones. Finally, ensure that everybody can manage crises. Great teams have many people who make good quality decisions when under pressure.

• SUCCESS

"When you have completed 80% of the job, there is only 80% left" is a good guideline. Poor math, perhaps, but it indicates the emotional hill that must be climbed. Finishing is an art: some people are fine finishers, while others have difficulty completing a book, building a house or shipping a product. Keep people's eyes on the goal. Make good decisions and put together delivery teams that reach their destination. Ensure that people follow good habits. If possible, encourage them to enjoy the journey as well as reaching the goal. Satisfy your sponsors and deliver the agreed picture of perfection.

Super Teams often go a step further and become 'A Class Act.' How to make this happen? Start by ensuring that everybody has the character, competence and consistency required to fulfill his or her role in the team. Building on this platform, encourage people to express their creativity and add that touch of class. If appropriate, you might also want the team to become Pacesetters. Such teams have a different kind of psychology. They take the lead, maintain the lead and extend the lead. Pacesetters make the new rules for the game. What is the next step after you have finished? Share your knowledge with others, then move onto the next fulfilling challenge. If appropriate, repeat the process for building a Super Team.

How to use this book? You can work through it as a leader and, if you wish, do the exercises with your team. Great educators often follow the Three I's: Inspiration, Implementation and Integration.

First, they create an inspiring environment where people can learn.

Second, they provide implementation tools that work.

Third, they help people to integrate the learning into their daily lives.

The Super Teams Book aims to follow a similar process. If you wish, start by tackling the exercise called *The Key Challenges*. Then, when reading the book, look for ideas you can use to resolve these issues. Chapter 1 concentrates on laying the foundations for the team. Chapter 2 provides practical tools for guiding people to success. Take the ideas you like and use them to build your Super Team

THE KEY CHALLENGES

The key challenges I face in working to build a super team are:

- How to _____

  _____

  _____

  _____

- How to _____

  _____

  _____

  _____

- How to _____

  _____

  _____

  _____

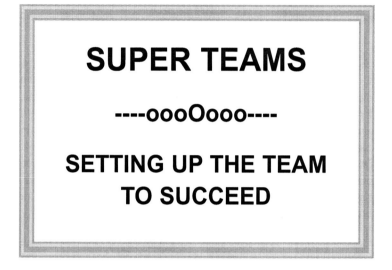

SUPER TEAMS

----oooOooo----

SETTING UP THE TEAM
TO SUCCEED

INTRODUCTION

Time to embark upon the adventure. How can you choose an exciting project? How can you make clear contracts with your sponsors? How can you deliver the picture of perfection?

"Enthusiasm and energy will take you a long way," said Paul, the turnaround leader, "but go into the role with your eyes open. Load the dice to increase your chances of success. Military missions often fail, for example, because they are imprecise and open-ended. Guerrilla wars and one-off strikes have their own logic: but long-term campaigns depend on public support. Similar rules apply to teamwork. Set crystal clear goals and get the right backup. Get in, get the job done and get on to the next mission. Perhaps the biggest challenge, however, is to create a second-generation super team. That calls for taking the tough decisions required to sustain long-term results."

Imagine you have been invited to lead a project. The first step is to create the right conditions for success. This rule applies whether you are starting a new team, taking over a business or facilitating a turnaround. Start by taking 'Time Out' to reflect and gather information. Here are some points to consider before accepting the position.

You can make sure you want to lead a team

Take a step back for a moment. Start by asking yourself the obvious question: "Do I really want to lead the team?" Perhaps this is an opportunity to do brilliant work, but make sure it is the right vehicle. Desires ebb and flow. Sometimes you will enjoy leading a team, other times you will prefer being an individual contributor. Conditions will never be perfect, but try to catch the right wave at the right time.

"During the '90s, I loved leading teams," said Diane, a forensic scientist. "Private companies threatened our traditional work for the police. Like all government agencies, we were forced to adjust to the new world, and I was invited to ensure our laboratory became more 'commercial.' Leading the (scientists) proved to be 'interesting.' Fortunately we managed to retain our professional integrity while also producing a 'profit.' Today I am concentrating on individual research. Given the right opportunity, however, I would grasp the chance to lead a dedicated team."

Reflect for a moment. Will taking the role be the right move forward? Double-check by tackling the exercise called *My Vocation*. Your vocation is your calling – it is what you are here to do – which may be expressed in a recurring life-theme. For example, the 'red thread' in your life may be encouraging people, building businesses, solving problems, making the world a better place or whatever. Your vocation remains constant but, over the years, you will employ different vehicles for expressing it on the way towards doing valuable work. Beware – some people fall in love with the vehicle, such as gaining status, and forget their vocation. Bear in mind also that there are different kinds of leadership. You can shape the future by writing a book, building a positive prototype or whatever. Make sure that taking the role is the best way to employ your talents. If the answer is 'Yes,' then move onto the next stage.

You can find the right opportunity to be a leader

Choose a project that puts a spring in your step. What for you would be the best vehicle? Would you prefer to work with a 'Start-Up Team,' a 'Turnaround Team' or a 'Maintenance Team'? How to find the right leadership possibility? Three rules are worth considering.

a) Choose the sponsor carefully

People work best with kindred spirits. Whenever possible, work for somebody who is a vocational soul mate. Choose a sponsor with whom you have a values fit and who shares similar high professional standards.

"My old boss kept asking me to join his new business," explained Karen, a senior manager. "Eventually I joined him to direct the company's People Strategy. Why? 'Respect' is the first word that comes to mind. We can have a dialogue because we are on the same wavelength. Decision-making then becomes simpler, especially when we encounter stormy weather."

How to find such a sponsor? Keep in touch with your network: maintain contact with the people with whom you might like to work in the future. "But what if I don't know the potential employer?" you may ask. Research them in great detail. Discover if they live their stated values, especially when under pressure. Build up a full picture to ensure it is not a 'blind date.'

b) Choose the culture carefully.

Ask yourself a tough question: "Will I enjoying working in this place, even if my sponsor leaves?" Choose an environment that is exciting and gives you energy. Remember also that there are 'cultures' within a culture. Be particularly careful, for example, if you are a 'pioneering type' who likes working in 'Rising Businesses,' rather than a 'Dying Businesses.'

Why? Great companies often begin by being 80% Spirit and 20% System. Upon reaching a certain size, however, they must provide customers with a predictable experience. So they reverse the balance, going for 80% System and 20% Spirit. (See illustration on page 19.) Such companies still attract people who want to shape the future, but leveraging the 'cash cow' calls for hiring a different kind of person. They need people who enjoy putting replicable processes into place that others can follow. Pioneers can then help to take the business onto the next curve. Great employers hire the right kinds of people in the right parts of the business at the right stage of their evolution. Find the niche where you can do fulfilling work that also benefits the employer.

c) Choose the project carefully.

Leaders must generate enthusiasm, so find a venture that gives you energy. Try tackling the exercise called *My Leadership Opportunity*. Clarify how to find or create the right opening. One final point, especially if you are 'adrenalin-driven,' choose a challenge that you 'respect.' Why? Mountaineers must respect the mountain; otherwise they become sloppy, which is dangerous. Leaders must also respect the task. They are then more likely to remain 'alert' and perform brilliantly.

THE COMPANY CURVE

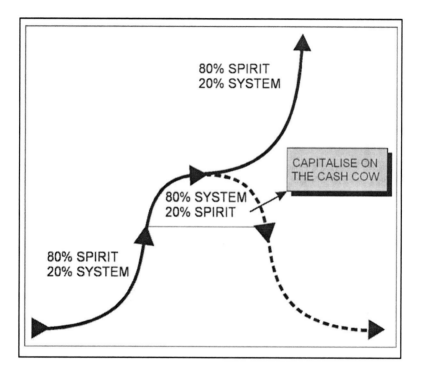

You can clarify the sponsor's Picture of Perfection

Look at the world from the sponsor's point of view. What challenges do they face? What results do they want delivered? Research this in detail before meeting the potential employers. Start by tackling two exercises. The first is called *Satisfying The Key Sponsors*. Ask yourself: "Who are the key sponsors? What are their burning issues? What is their picture of success?" Sounds simple, but it can be complex if you have several sponsors, all with different agendas and management styles. Some may focus on the overall vision, while others prefer minute detail. You must show each person that you understand the challenges and can deliver the goods.

Start from your destination and work backwards. Tackle the exercise called *Success: The Actual Words People Will Be Saying*. Write the names of everybody the team must satisfy: the key sponsor, managers and individual customers. Pick a date in the future, such as in 12 months time. Write the 'Actual Words' you want people to be saying then about the team's performance. For example, you may want the sponsor to say: "The customers are giving stunning feedback. The team always fulfills its promises. Three people have been promoted from it in the last year." How can you do your best to ensure they are saying these things? Clarify your strategies for making this happen.

You can rate the team's chances of success

Take an honest look at the task ahead and tackle the exercise called *Success Rating*. On a scale 0 to 10, how highly do you judge the team's chances of reaching its goals? Make sure the odds are at least 7/10. (Of course, much depends on your willingness to gamble. Some people like to start with low expectations and produce miracles. Depends on your own preference, but at least be aware of the odds.) What must happen to boost the team's chances? Be specific. You may want to get the required resources, choose your own management team, agree on the degrees of autonomy, etc. Clarify these issues in your own mind before meeting the sponsors. Good leaders do everything possible to create the right foundation for success. Let's explore how this works in practice. (Some of you may have read the following example in *The Magic of Work*. If so, move onto the next section.)

Dave, a rising soccer manager, calculated the odds when considering his future job opportunities. Three clubs in the top division had offered him interviews for the vacant post of manager. Researching the clubs in turn, he found that each Board of Directors wanted him to achieve similar goals. These were:

1) to build a team that finished tenth or higher in the league and competed seriously in the postseason

2) to play good football that attracted an average attendance of 70,000 over the season

3) to ensure the club remained financially solvent.

Dave considered the resources required to achieve such results, then rated the chances of success. Club A were moving into a new stadium. Few transfer funds would be available and, furthermore, the Board insisted he retain the present backroom staff. He rated the chances of success as 3/10. Club B had also borrowed money to rebuild its stadium. Some transfer funds were available, but these fell far short of the kitty required to significantly improve the team. Chances of Success: 5/10. Club C had a track record of providing 'freedom to manage' and a large transfer fund. Chances of Success: 7/10. Focusing on this final opportunity, Dave considered what must be done to boost the chances to 10/10.

MY LEADERSHIP OPPORTUNITY

The Leadership Opportunity I am looking for is one where I am able:

- to _____
- to _____
- to _____

The steps I can take to create such a leadership opportunity are:

- to _____
- to _____
- to _____

SATISFYING THE KEY SPONSORS

This exercise invites you to do three things. First: Write the names of each sponsor the team must satisfy. (This page provides space for one sponsor. Take a separate page for each one.) Second: Write the specific results that each sponsor wants delivered. Third: Write what the team can do to satisfy each of these sponsors.

The sponsor's name is:

● _____

The results they want delivered are:

● _____

● _____

● _____

The specific things we can do to satisfy this sponsor are:

● _____

● _____

● _____

SUCCESS - The actual words people will be saying about the team

1. The specific date we want to be looking back from is:

● _____

The actual words we want the following groups to be saying are:

The MD

● _____

● _____

● _____

The key sponsor

● _____

● _____

● _____

The customers

● _____

● _____

● _____

The team members

- _____
- _____
- _____

Other groups

- _____
- _____
- _____

2. The specific things we can do to help ensure people are saying these things are:

- _____
- _____
- _____

3. The things we can do to get some early successes along the way are:

- _____
- _____
- _____

You can clarify what you can control

Everybody enjoys having a sense of autonomy. Before taking the leadership role, clarify to what extent you will be able to shape the team's destiny. Try tackling the exercise called *Controlling The Controllables*. Looking at the potential project, list three things. First, describe what you can control. For example, your attitude, professional standards, selecting the team, etc. Second, describe what you can't control. For example, the sponsor's personality, the market, the customers, etc. Third, describe how to maximize what you can control and manage what you can't control.

Bearing these findings in mind, will you have enough freedom?

"Sports people do everything in their power to win," said Dave, "but the outcome may still lie in the lap of the Gods. Roger Black, for example, ran out of his skin to gain the 400 meters silver medal in the Atlanta Olympics. On any other occasion, Roger may have won the gold, but he competed against the remarkable Michael Johnson. My approach is to maximize the chances of achieving success."

Dave considered the 'controllables' offered in each manager's position. Club A offered limited scope. While able to coach and pick the team, his hands were tied on transfers. The Board also insisted he keep the present backroom staff, some of whom he did not rate. Club B offered larger transfer funds, but still lacked the cash to build a Top 10 Team. Club C provided the greatest opportunity. Providing he made clear contracts, he could recruit his own management team, buy good players and play the manager's role without interference. Dave began focusing on his chosen option.

You can decide whether you want to take the leadership opportunity

Time to make a decision. Bearing in mind your answers to the previous questions: Do you want to embark upon the leadership challenge? Does it put a spring in your step? What will be the upsides and downsides? How can you maximize the pluses and minimize the minuses? Tackle the exercise on this theme called *My Motivation For Leading The Team*. Rate how excited you feel about tackling the

challenge. If the score is 7 or less, be careful. You might still hold an exploratory meeting with the sponsors, but recognize what must be in place for you to consider the role. If the score is 7+, look at how to boost the rating. Clarify the steps that must be taken to make it 10/10.

SUCCESS RATING: Rating The Team's Chances Of Success

My present assessment of the team's chances of delivering success is: _____/10

The specific things that must be done to increase the team's chances of success are:

● to _____

● to _____

● to _____

The specific things I should do before taking the role ro ensure the team has the greatest chance of success are:

● to _____

● to _____

● to _____

CONTROLLING THE CONTROLLABLES

CAN CONTROL - The things we can control:

● We can control _____

_____

● We can control _____

_____

● We can control _____

_____

● We can control _____

_____

● We can control _____

_____

CAN'T CONTROL - The things we can't control:

● We can't control _____

_____

● We can't control _____

_____

● We can't control _____

_____

CONTROLLING THE CONTROLLABLES - Action plan

The specific things we can do to build on what we can control, and manage what we can't control, are:

● We can _____

_____

● We can _____

_____

● We can _____

_____

MY MOTIVATION FOR LEADING THE TEAM

The team's goals are:

- to _____

- to _____

- to _____

The PLUSES of leading the team will be:

- _____   • _____

- _____   • _____

- _____   • _____

The MINUSES of leading the team will be:

- _____   • _____

- _____   • _____

- _____   • _____

My motivation rating for leading the team is: _____/10

Dave decided that Club C provided the best opportunity to put his principles into practice. Should he still pursue the manager roles at Clubs A and B? "Never say no straight away," he explained. "Get lots of information, then make a decision." Playing fair, however, he informed each club he would be attending other interviews. He promised to give a decision within 48 hours of meeting each Board. Dave did not want to burn any bridges, but felt it was vital to join the right setup. Club C remained his first choice, but he did not feel desperate. Fresh opportunities would arise as the new season brought managerial casualties. He looked forward to the interviews. Time to take the next step.

You can prepare properly for your meeting with the potential sponsors

Mentally rehearse your meeting with the sponsors. Prepare by focusing on the areas of Credibility, Clarity, Concrete Results and Contracting. Ask yourself: "How can I establish credibility? How to be clear about their picture of perfection? How to show that I will deliver concrete results? Assuming all goes well, how can I make clear working contracts with the sponsors?" Credibility can be established, for example, by showing that you understand the world from the sponsor's point of view. Demonstrate that you also recognize the challenges facing the team. If possible, show how you would get some early successes.

Looking ahead to the interviews with each club, Dave rehearsed his plan. He needed to:

- be warm, friendly and demonstrate his football knowledge, thus confirming his reputation for possessing both people-management skills and technical coaching ability

- show respect to the employers, but also ensure he covered his agenda during the meeting

- demonstrate his belief in the club, but also show he understood the playing and financial challenges it was facing

- clarify the Directors' goals for the club: the results they wanted delivered both on and off the field, then 'play back' the goals to show he understood their ambitions

- share his goals for the team and reassure the Directors that he would get some early successes towards achieving these targets

- if appropriate, declare that he was extremely interested in the management position. He would quickly get back to the Directors with a concrete proposal on how to achieve the club's goals

- explain his approach to the job, ask if it was okay to be honest, to outline his way of working and to describe the resources required to reach the goals.

Dave wanted to cover the following points. First, he looked forward to the possibility of managing the club, but also had two other offers. Second, if the Directors wanted him to become manager, he would need certain resources. He would appoint his own management team, require a substantial transfer budget, etc. Third, he had certain management beliefs. During the first months, the 'established' players might challenge his authority. At this point, he would make his 'rules' clear; the players must decide whether or not to opt-in. (He would have already lined up better replacements for those players who chose to move on.)

- conclude the meeting in a positive way.

Dave planned to reassure the Directors. He would write a proposal for taking the team forward and get it back to them within 48 hours. The plan would highlight some 'early wins' that could be achieved to boost the fans' confidence, thus improving season ticket sales. Specific milestones would be set for achieving the medium and long term goals. The Directors would obviously then decide whether or not they wanted him to become manager.

(Dave was offered all three posts. He opted for the club where the Directors were decisive; they enthusiastically provided the resources on the spot.)

You can meet with your potential sponsors

Time to meet the sponsors. Get the first few minutes right and, if appropriate, establish credibility. Do this in a way that feels natural for you. One approach is to show you understand the challenges facing the business. Clarify the results the sponsor wants delivered. Play back the picture to ensure you agree on the 'What.' Describe how you would deliver the short, medium and long-term goals. If the sponsors invite you to take the leadership role, move onto the next stage. Clear contracting is vital in any relationship, especially when providing services to a sponsor. At the end of the contracting process, make sure that everybody has matching pictures about:

a) **what mountain you are climbing** – the specific results to be delivered

b) **why you are climbing it** – the benefits to the business

c) **how you can climb it** – the rules to follow and the autonomy you will have to do things in your own way

d) **what resources you will need** – the support required to do the job

e) **when you will reach the summit** – the specific dates when results must be delivered.

Reassure your sponsors. Show that you recognize potential problems that may be on their 'Radar.' 'But I want them to trust me,' you may say. Forget it. As one MD put it: "I believe in certainty, not trust. When the Red Arrows turn right, they know everybody has turned right." During the early days, you will remain on trial. Sponsors will visit your part of the business and 'jump on the floor boards' to see if they are shaky. Ensure they don't find problems; otherwise they will meddle and make your life a misery. Finally, ask how they would want to be kept up-to-date. Proactively keeping them informed is a good way to create the time and space to get on with the job.

You can put forward a proposal for delivering the results

Assuming the meeting goes well, the next step is to put the matching pictures on paper. Conclude by saying you will get back to the sponsors within 48 hours with a specific action plan. The proposal should include:

- the agreed picture of success.
- the benefits to the business
- the autonomy you need to deliver the results.
- the early successes you will deliver.

- the way you will keep your sponsors informed.

What if the meeting is difficult? The relationship may be disastrous; the goalposts may shift; the support may not be forthcoming. Don't be afraid to ask for time to reflect. Buy time by explaining that you will respond with a proposal. If you then decide to take the role, get back with an action plan.

What if you decide to say "No, thanks?" Engineer a positive exit. Try to be diplomatic, because you may encounter these potential sponsors in the future. If you commit yourself to reaching the targets, however, move on to the next stage. Let's explore how you can lead the team to success.

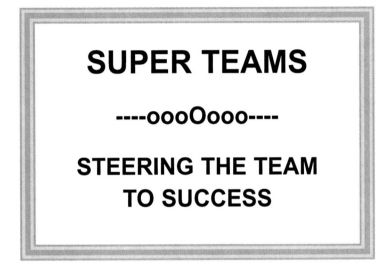

SUPER TEAMS

----oooOooo----

STEERING THE TEAM
TO SUCCESS

INTRODUCTION

Time to get the show on the road. How can you build the team? How can you recruit the right soul players and star players? How can you ensure people want to achieve the picture of perfection? How can you lead the team to success?

This chapter starts by focusing on **Spirit: The Heartbeat of the Team.** It then provides practical tools that you can use to:

1) build on the team's STRENGTHS

2) clarify the team's SPECIFIC GOALS

3) clarify the team's STRATEGY

4) ensure the team delivers STAR PERFORMANCES

5) provide the team members with SUPPORT

6) tackle challenges and find creative SOLUTIONS

7) ensure that the team achieves SUCCESS.

How to move forward? The following pages offer exercises you can use either by yourself or with your team members. You can employ these in one-to-one sessions or, for example, on an 'Away Day.' "But what if I am taking over an existing team?" you may ask. The same principles apply, but the practice is more challenging. Decisive leadership will be required, because the old rules will be established. Build on the best of the past, but give people clear messages about the future culture. Let's start by exploring the driving force behind the Super Team.

SPIRIT:
The Heartbeat Of The Team

"Get the right people with the right attitude" is the maxim. Great teams are made up of people who have 'similarity of spirit and diversity of strengths.' Visitors notice that there is a buzz in the building. They ask: 'What are these people on? Can we bottle it to take back to our place?' Hire energetic people who go that extra mile to persuade you they can contribute to the mission. Attitude plus ability equals achievement. 'Where do you find such people?' somebody may ask. Start by creating a compelling vision – you will find that many then beat a path to your door. You can find others by using ideas described later in this chapter. Belief plus behavior produces the bottom-line results. Never compromise on character, otherwise you will hit problems.

> "Ten years ago I made a big mistake," explained Dave, the football manager. 'The non-league club I led looked certain to gain promotion, but then I took a gamble. Aiming to seal the title, I paid a large transfer fee for a gifted player who, at that level, was magical. Scouts told me he was a moaner but, being arrogant, I thought I could 'change' him. The honeymoon lasted a month. One day after training, I found him at the pub, telling players how 'everything was wrong' at the club. He was holding court, bragging about his exploits on the international scene. I immediately cancelled his contract. Certainly it cost us financially, but we still managed to get promotion. The experience taught me a lesson."

Times have changed. In the old world of work, organizations gave the message that it was acceptable to have negative people in a team. Leaders were expected to turn somersaults to 'motivate the unmotivated.' Teams often consisted of the following groups of people:

* 20% were Super Positive.
* 60% veered between being Positive, Neutral and Negative.
* 20% were Negative.

Today's world is different. We are all freelancers now. There are no safe jobs anymore; there are only 'projects.' Certainly the leader must still provide the right environment and encouragement. Nowadays, it is the team member's job to persuade the leader that he or she wants to be in the team, not the other way round. Life is a voluntary activity and people have to 'volunteer into' the team. So how do you start your recruitment drive?

You can clarify the team's spirit

'Taking responsibility' is the key competence in life. You want people who are self-managing and make their best contribution to the team. What other characteristics should they demonstrate? Start defining these qualities by tackling the exercise called *Spirit*. Give specific examples of how they might translate these into action. One leader outlined the major qualities he looked for in team members by saying, "I want people who are:

a) **positive** – they have a 'can do' attitude, add to the team's energy and are problem-solvers, rather than problem-makers
b) **professional** – they are technically competent, customer-focused and deliver on their promises
c) **peak performers** – they are outstanding in their particular field of expertise."

How to find good people? Begin considering the steps you can take in the areas of Recruitment, Reward and Retention. Hiring people can be like a blind date. Experienced applicants have mastered the art of shining in interviews. They also know how to give the 'right answers' in psychometric tests to fulfill the required profile. When in doubt, go back to your network. Recruit people you know, then build on their strengths and compensate for their weaknesses. Choose hungry people:

* who show the spirit you want in the team
* who show they have a good track record of decision-making and delivery

- who show they have taken the trouble to research the team's goals and picture of perfection.

Invite key team members to sit in on the sessions. Why? Three reasons:

- they must work with the new people
- they can explain to the applicant the spirit that is required in the team, thus reinforcing it in their own minds
- they can be present at the start of the contracting process.

Spirit is non-negotiable, but you are looking for characters, not clones. Give clear messages about the required results. Look for mutual benefits: clarify how reaching the goal will provide wins, both for themselves and the team. Invite them to reflect and get back to you as to whether or not they want to join the team.

How to retain good people? "Reward the behavior you want repeated" is the motto. Promote people who live the values. Offer people an annual 'Career Check' – like an annual health check – where they clarify their talents and future contribution to the business. Encourage people to take time out to reflect, rest and recover. Positive steps like these will only work if you have the right mix of people, however, which brings us to the next step.

SPIRIT

The spirit we would like people in the team to demonstrate is

(a) to _____

They would demonstrate this, for example, by:

● _____

(b) to _____

They would demonstrate this, for example, by:

● _____

(c) to _____

They would demonstrate this, for example, by:

● _____

(d) to _____

They would demonstrate this, for example, by:

● _____

RECRUITMENT – The things we can do to recruit people who demonstrate this spirit are:

- to _____
- to _____
- to _____

REWARD – the things we can do to reward people who demonstrate this spirit are:

- to _____
- to _____
- to _____

RETENTION – the things we can do to retain people who demonstrate this spirit are:

- to _____
- to _____
- to _____

can follow their successful patterns to deliver on future promises.

● Clarify their professional contribution

Repeat the team's picture of perfection. Clarify how the person can build on his or her strengths and help to achieve the vision. Certainly you will provide encouragement, but it is important for everybody to be proactive. Invite them to describe how they will make clear contracts with their sponsors, perform superb work and deliver success. Clarify how they will manage the 'fall-out' from any weaknesses. Settle on their best contribution to the business.

● Anticipate any potential problems

Many people "talk a good game." During the probation period, however, candidates will be judged by what they do, not by what they say. How do they make decisions, especially when under pressure? How do they translate these into action? Invite the person to look ahead to a potentially difficult scenario they may face in their work. Ask them to describe (a) the decision-making process they would go through, (b) the potential options they would consider and (c) the way they would then behave. Ask them to be super specific. Consider including some relevant role-playing at this point of the interview.

● Cover all the practical issues

Set aside time for the person to ask any questions concerning pay, conditions, trial period or other practical issues. Outline the next steps in the application process.

● Invite the applicant to write a proposal

Decide whether you want to hire the person. If the answer is 'Yes,' say you are interested in their taking the role. Invite the candidate to reflect and consider whether they want to join the team. If they choose to accept the offer, ask them to get back to you with a short proposal outlining the specific things they would aim to deliver in the first 6 months. They should also describe the support required to reach these goals.

Sounds like hard work? Yes, but selection is one of the most neglected factors in teamwork. Stay in touch with the newcomer during the probation period. Provide a great induction programme, early learning from positive models and the provision of a dedicated coach. Then you have a chance. Let's explore more of the qualities you can look for in candidates.

You can hire Achievers

How can you be a good talent spotter? How can you tell if people are hungry? How can you judge whether somebody will translate their potential into performance? The following pages outline one model you can use to identify Achievers. Success calls for finding people who align their own ambitions with those of the business. Again, you are looking to create a 'Win-Win.'

The **Achievement Model** is an approach you can use when hiring (or rehiring) people. Sports people employ it to focus on improving performance, but the principles can be applied in any field. The model outlines five steps that people take towards reaching their goals (see illustration). Here are some questions you can ask yourself – and the candidate – relating to each step on the road towards achievement. You can explore these themes when interviewing people.

THE ACHIEVEMENT MODEL

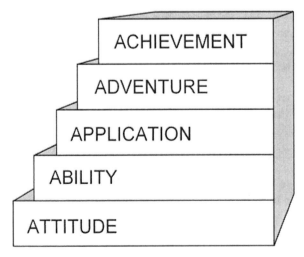

ACHIEVEMENT

ADVENTURE

APPLICATION

ABILITY

ATTITUDE

ATTITUDE

What is the person's attitude? Do they come across as being positive, negative, neutral or a mixture? Will they add to the team's energy? How do they fit with the spirit? Do they live in the realm of possibilities or problems? Are they 'creators,' 'consistents' or 'complainers'? Are they resilient? How do they react to setbacks – do they choose to succeed or sulk? Do they take responsibility? Can they give you three examples of where, when faced by a disappointment or operating in a vacuum situation, they took responsibility? What did they do then to shape the future? If they were asked to do pre-work, what was their approach? Was it professional, well thought-through or slapdash? *Rate their attitude on a scale 0 to 10.*

ABILITY

What are their top three strengths? What do they find fulfilling? When do they feel in their 'element'? What are the activities that give them energy? Where do they quickly see patterns? Where do they balance seeming paradoxes, being able to simultaneously see both the details and the vision? When are they able to be both 'hands-on' and 'helicoptering'? When are they are good finishers?

Looking back at their personal and professional accomplishments, what have been their most satisfying 'projects'? Exploring one or two 'projects' in turn, what did they do right then to achieve success? How can they follow these patterns in the future? *Bearing in mind their potential role in the team, rate their ability to perform it on a scale 0 to 10.*

APPLICATION

Discipline is one of the keys to delivery. You need people who are hard working and consistent. What are the activities in which they are naturally self-managing? Where do they love to follow the daily disciplines? Where do they enjoy the journey as much as reaching the goal? What are the areas in which they have high professional standards?

Thinking about working in an organization, would they be good at managing their sponsors? Would they make clear contracts with people, keep them informed and deliver on their promises? Would they be proactive in managing upwards? *Bearing in mind their potential role in the team, rate their application in this area on a scale 0 to 10.*

ADVENTURE

When do they use their imagination? When do they take creative initiatives? Where do they have good 'personal radar'? When do they anticipate what is 'going to happen before it happens'? Is it in the field of technology, people-management, sales or whatever? When are they strategic? What are the activities in which they quickly see the destination, the results to be delivered? When do they go 'AB … Z'? Where do they have gaps in their repertoire? What might be the consequences of these gaps? *Bearing in mind the role for which they are applying, rate their capacity for adventure on a scale 0 to 10.*

ACHIEVEMENT

What are the activities where they consistently deliver As, rather than Bs or Cs? Where do they have the ability to be peak performers? Returning to look at their past achievements, what did they finish successfully? What did they do right then? How can they follow similar principles in the future? How high is their ambition? What are their goals, personally and professionally? Are they aware of the pluses and minuses involved in achieving their goals? Are they willing to accept the whole package? Where can they be a brilliant niche provider? If you were an MD, what would you specifically hire them to deliver? Assuming they want to join the team, how do they plan to fulfill their contribution to the business? What resources will they require to make this happen? *Bearing these answers in mind, rate the likelihood of them delivering successfully. Do this on a scale 0 to 10.*

Such questions are just a starting point. Expand on those that you feel are useful for discovering more about potential team members. One other factor may be worth considering.

You can recruit people whose comfort zone is success

"Comfort Zones get a bad press," said Dave, the football manager. "Great players, like (Peyton Manning), are only comfortable when performing at their best. Average players, on the other hand, are comfortable turning in average performances. They accept a 50/50 split between winning and losing. Poor players feel comfortable with being beaten. Some actually get worried when leading in a game and want the opposition to score. Why? The burden of expectation is lifted and they feel at ease again. When scouting for players, I look for the zone in which they feel at ease. Successful teams are made up of players who feel comfortable winning."

Star Performers always want to give their best, because falling short of their standards causes pain. Setbacks reveal their true character. They are resilient and show remarkable powers of recovery. Recruit people who flourish when faced by high demands – such as tackling a crisis, making a keynote speech or presenting to difficult customers. "Pressure, what pressure?" they say. "You enjoy these moments. They force you to pull out all the stops." Great teams have great players who produce great performances on great occasions. How many such people do you have in your team? Who deliver the goods when it matters?

You can build the Super Team

Imagine you are starting with a blank sheet of paper. Who would you hire? Write the names of the people you would immediately recruit. "But what if I am taking over an existing group?" you may ask. Providing you have contracted properly with your sponsors – and got their back-up – follow the same principles. Dedicated professionals will have nothing to fear. They will be first on your team sheet. Semi-detached players who perform at half-speed may try to set the rules, but it is your head that is on the block. You will live or die by the efforts of people in your team.

Tackle the exercise called *Building My Team*. Begin by writing three lists. First, the people you *definitely* want. Some may already be in the team, others you may need to hire. Second, the people you may want. Third, the people you *do not want* in the team. Compile your action plan.

Looking at each group in turn, describe three things. First, the steps you can take to get the people you definitely want. Second, the steps you can take with the people you may want. Third, the steps you can take with people you don't want in the team. Get the right people with the right spirit lays the foundations for success.

Quickly set the tone. Bring in people who demonstrate the new culture. They will act as positive models and reinforce the 'rules.' Never walk past a quality problem. People will be looking at what you do, not what you say. If 'old timers' try to undermine your authority, act fairly but decisively, sooner rather than later. Give them the opportunity to go away, reflect and choose their way forward. Everybody has choices and, of course, every choice has consequences. Super Teams work best when everybody takes responsibility for opting-in every second of every day.

You can quickly develop the spirit

Getting enthusiastic people is vital, but there are many other steps you can take to develop a positive culture. "Change the physical things to change the psychological things" is a good rule to remember. Try tackling the exercise called *Spirit: My Action Plan*. You can, for example:

- **go for some quick visible wins**
  Take care of all the 'hygiene factors,' such as providing competitive salaries, access to health care, offering educational opportunities, etc. Provide a stimulating and attractive work place. Give people the resources required to do the job. Develop a superb induction programme. Ensure that new people learn "the way we do things around here" by spending time with positive models during their first month.

- **make sure everybody knows the team's goals: display these throughout the building**
  Peak performers wake up in the morning and concentrate on their A1 Goals. Focusing can be more difficult in teams, because people may pursue their own agendas. Ensure everybody can 'see' the team's vision – plus the benefits to themselves, the customers and the company.

- **communicate the team's progress towards achieving the goals**
  Employ many different kinds of media – such as newsletters, emails, Away Days, update sessions – to communicate 'weekly wins' and success stories. Start each meeting by reporting on

milestones that have been passed. Conclude the meetings by ensuring that everybody's action plans are related to achieving the goals.

● **keep in touch with your people**
The 'Personal Touch' is vital. Spend quality time with each person. Ask them about (a) their successes, (b) their goals for the next month, (c) the support they require to do the job and (d) any other topics they would like to discuss. Get to know their possible future options and professional ambitions. Explore ways they can presently harness their emotional energy to achieve the team's goals.

● **ensure somebody becomes the "custodian of the spirit."**
Certainly it is everybody's job to nurture the ethos. You cannot, for example, 'delegate' values. Show you are serious, however, by appointing somebody to become the "custodian of the spirit." Such a person must have widespread credibility, because it is a tough job. The positive parts are obvious. For example, they can publicize success stories and spot future stars.

The 'truth-telling' part is more difficult. For example, sometimes they might suggest ways the leadership team can be even better at living the values. Presenting such ideas calls for three things. First, courage. Second, clear contracting with the sponsors that it is okay to tell the truth. Third, communication skills. They must have the ability to present difficult messages in a way that people can accept. Positive 'Truth Tellers' are invaluable, however, if the team is to progress.

Spirit is the driving force. Conclude this section by describing the specific things you can do to develop the right culture. Creating a stimulating environment is the starting point, but much more is required to achieve success. The following pages describe seven steps you can take to steer the team towards its picture of perfection. Let's explore the first step.

BUILDING THE TEAM

The people I **do want** in the team are:

- _____
- _____
- _____
- _____
- _____

- _____
- _____
- _____
- _____
- _____

The people I **may want** in the team are:

- _____
- _____
- _____

- _____
- _____
- _____

The people I **do not want** in the team are:

- _____
- _____
- _____

- _____
- _____
- _____

MY ACTION PLAN

The specific steps I can take with the people I want in the team are:

- I can _____
- I can _____
- I can _____

The specific steps I can take with the people I may want in the team are:

- I can _____
- I can_____
- I can _____

The specific steps I can take with the people I do not want in the team are:

- I can _____
- I can_____
- I can _____

SPIRIT: ACTION PLAN

The specific things we can do to ensure that we have the right spirit in the team are:

● to _____

_____

_____

● to _____

_____

_____

● to _____

_____

_____

Step One

BUILD ON THE TEAM'S
STRENGTHS

INTRODUCTION

Great leaders capitalize on their people's talents. If you managed the No. 48 Hendrick Motorsports team, you would encourage Jimmie Johnson to concentrate on driving, rather than becoming a mechanic. If you managed ABBA, you would encourage Agneta and Frida to sing, Bjorn and Benny to write the songs, not the other way round. If you ran Bletchley Park during the Second World War, you would encourage Alan Turing to crack code, rather than fight on the front line with a rifle. If you led a start up business, you would urge the brilliant sales person to get even more customers, not to spend 20 hours a week programming computers. Why? Capitalizing on your assets provides the greatest chance of success.

Star Performers and Survivors have one thing in common, they define themselves in terms of their strengths, not their 'sicknesses.' Survivors say things like: "I am a strong person who has these talents – I just happen to have an illness at the moment." They define themselves as people, not patients. Star Performers maximize their talents and also balance apparent contradictions. They say things like: "When doing work I love, I see both the overall vision and every detail. Everything slows down, but my reactions are faster than those of people around me." Building on strengths does not mean ignoring the 'fall out' from weaknesses; it means finding ways to compensate. World Class performers are extremists: they make extreme use of their gifts.

How can you harness people's talents? Positive Modeling is the greatest strength – so build a leadership team that will act as good models. Great leaders recognize that they are always 'on stage,' so they must practice what they preach. They must live the values, translate these into a clear vision and ensure people deliver visible results. Build on your own strengths as a leader, but surround yourself with complementary skills. Get people who can fill the roles of Energizer, Environmentalist and Executor. Energizers provide the inspiring vision. Environmentalists provide the climate in which self-managing people can grow. Executors make sure the work gets completed. Clarify the entire Super Team's assets by identifying each

62

person's top talents. Ask yourself: "Where do they consistently produce A's, rather than B's or C's?" Compile the *Strengths Inventory*, identify the gaps and get these filled. Let's explore each of these steps.

You can recognize the strength of positive modeling

"Positive modeling is vital," explained one MD. "Senior managers set the tone. People watch what they do, not what they say." Build a leadership team that will encourage people to use their talents. Leaders, like parents, create the climate. They must live the message, otherwise it gets diluted. After finalizing the core team, agree on their code of conduct. Invite them to tackle the exercise call *Positive Modeling*. They are to describe the Dos and Don'ts involved in being good models. Encourage them to avoid theory or management jargon – preferably giving specific examples. Leaders must focus on their 'behavior' – not their intentions – because this is what others see. So how can you assemble a good leadership team? Let's begin by focusing on your own talents.

You can build on your strengths as a leader

Capitalize on your natural leadership style. Everybody has been a good leader at some point during his or her life. You may have managed a rock group, captained a football team, organized a charity event or led a turnaround business. Tackle the exercise called *My Successful Leadership Style*. Looking back over the years, identify two occasions when you led a good team. Exploring each example in turn, describe three things. First, describe what you did right as a leader. Second, describe what you could have done better. Third, describe how you can apply these lessons when leading your present team.

Build on what you do well, but compensate for weaknesses. Translate these principles into practice by tackling the exercise called *My Strengths As A Leader*. First, describe your top three leadership talents. Second, describe the implications of these qualities. You may inspire people with your vision, for example, but neglect chasing the daily tasks. Allowing for this downside, you would require a good co-ordinator. Third, describe your best contribution as a leader. Playing to your own strengths is crucial, but graduate beyond being a one-man

POSITIVE modeling

DO'S - The specific things that we can do to act as positive models are:

- _____
- _____
- _____
- _____
- _____

DON'TS - The specific things we should not do if we are to act as positive models are:

- _____
- _____
- _____
- _____
- _____

MY SUCCESSFUL LEADERSHIP STYLE

Looking back on your life, think of two occasions when you led a team successfully. (These can be in any area of life.) Considering each example in turn, describe: a) the things you did right and, b) the things you could have done better. Then consider how to apply this learning to your next leadership challenge.

First example - the time when I led a team successfully was:

● when I _____

The things I did right when I was leading the team were:

● _____

● _____

● _____

The things I could have done better when leading the team were:

● _____

● _____

● _____

Second example - the time when I led a team successfully was:

● when I _____

The things I did right when I was leading the team were:

● _____

● _____

● _____

The things I could have done better when leading the team were:

● _____

● _____

● _____

Bearing this learning in mind, the things I can do to lead the team successfully are:

● _____

● _____

● _____

MY STRENGTHS AS A LEADER

What are your strengths as a leader? What are the
implications of these strengths? What people do you need
around you to build a good leadership team? Bearing
these answers in mind, what will be your best contribution
as a leader?

My top three strengths as a leader are:

- I can _____
- I can _____
- I can _____

The implications of my strengths as a leader are:

- that _____
- that _____
- that _____

Bearing in mind my strengths, my best contributions as a
leader will be:

- to _____
- to _____
- to _____

You can build a great leadership team

Create a positive team at the core. Get people who fill the roles of Energizer, Environmentalist and Executor. Energizers communicate an exciting vision. Environmentalists create an encouraging climate in which self-managing people perform great work. Executors ensure the tasks get completed. Leaders often possess all three qualities, but teams work best with clear demarcation lines. Energizers who dip down into execution, for example, can cause chaos.

How does your leadership team rate on the Three Es? Try tackling the exercise on this theme. First, on a scale 0 to 10, rate them as Energizers, Environmentalists and Executors. Second, describe what they do well in each area, plus what they can do better. Successful companies, for example, often follow a certain pattern. During their early days, they score highly on Energy and Execution, lower on Environment. People are hooked on adrenalin and feel they are making a difference. As companies mature, however, individual agendas change. People still love work, but want more autonomy, rather than less. They also want a better 'life-balance,' searching for fulfillment in both their personal and professional lives. Companies can retain such people by building an encouraging environment. Third, make an action plan for improving each of the Three E's. Then go onto the next step.

Settle on the people who are required at the hub. Tackle the exercise called *Building A Superb Leadership Team*. First, describe again your leadership strengths. Second, describe the complementary strengths needed around you. Third, put together your action plan for building the leadership team.

Dave the football manager, for example, hired a Number Two who was an Environmentalist. Despite being a good people-manager himself, he could not devote the time required for one-to-one relationships with 30 players. Football clubs easily revert to old-style, blame cultures. Players then shrink into their shells or hit out. Dave brought in an Assistant Manager who focused on maintaining a positive environment in the club.

You can build on people's strengths

Every person has talents: but how to identify their gifts? Start by asking everybody in the team to clarify what they do brilliantly. Invite them to tackle the exercise called *My Super Strengths*. They are to describe three things. First, their top three talents. Second, the specific 'projects' and other activities that interest and give them energy right now. Third, bearing in mind their answers, what they believe will be their best contribution. People are to define this in terms of 'Deliverables.' They must outline the benefits – for themselves, for the team and for the company. Then meet each person to finalize their best role in the business. (Many other tools for clarifying people's strengths can be found in *The Magic of Work*.)

"Giving my team this exercise produced several business benefits," reported one MD. "Carol, the IT Manager, saw her major talent as technical problem solving. She loves tackling leading edge challenges, however, rather than doing 'maintenance work' inside our own building. Carol is also skilled at people management, particularly with external customers. Following on from our conversation, she developed a role in the field. She now works off-site with three demanding customers, helping them to shape their future IT strategy. Several benefits have emerged: cash, contact with leading edge customers, and more creative work for Carol."

THE THREE Es - RATING THE LEADERSHIP TEAM

Excellent leadership teams often score highly in the areas of being Energizers, Environmentalists and Executors. This exercise invites you to do two things. First, to rate your present leadership team's performance in each of these areas. Do this on a scale 0 to 10. Second, to describe what the team does well and can do better in each of these areas.

ENERGIZERS

Rate the leadership team's performance in energizing people. For example, by providing an exciting and inspiring vision.

0 1 2 3 4 5 6 7 8 9 10

ENVIRONMENTALISTS

Rate the leadership team's performance in providing an encouraging environment in which self-managing people can perform at their best.

0 1 2 3 4 5 6 7 8 9 10

EXECUTORS

Rate the leadership team's performance in making things happen and getting things done.

0 1 2 3 4 5 6 7 8 9 10

ENERGIZERS

The specific things we do well are:

- _____

- _____

- _____

The specific things we can do better are:

- _____

- _____

ENVIRONMENTALISTS

The specific things we do well are:

- _____

- _____

- _____

The specific things we can do better are:

- _____

- _____

EXECUTERS

The specific things we do well are:

- _____

- _____

- _____

The specific things we can do better are:

- _____

- _____

THE THREE Es - the action plan

Bearing these answers in mind, the specific things we want to do are:

- _____

- _____

- _____

BUILDING A SUPERB LEADERSHIP TEAM

The strengths that I have as a leader are that I am able:

- to _____
- to _____
- to _____

The complementary strengths I need to add to the leadership team are people who are able:

- to _____
- to _____
- to _____

The specific steps I can take towards making this happen and building a good leadership team are:

- to _____
- to _____
- to _____

MY SUPER STRENGTHS

My top three strengths are:

- I can _____
- I can _____
- I can _____

The specific kinds of ' projects' & activities that interest me and give me energy right now are:

- _____
- _____
- _____

Bearing these answwers in mind, my best contribution to the business would be:

- _____
- _____
- _____

You can ask 'The Freelance Question' about people's contribution to the team

Imagine you take over a team. How can you judge whether somebody will be an asset or a liability? Providing people buy into the spirit, everybody will be given a chance to deliver the goods. Decisions must be taken on an ongoing basis, however, not just about those people you inherit, but about everybody in the team. Leaders are paid to make such tough calls, so try tackling the exercise called *The Freelance Question.* Write the name of every person in your team. Focusing on each one in turn, consider three things.

- If this person left to go freelance and offered his or her services back to the team, would you hire them? Yes or No? If the answer is 'Yes,' continue onto the next stage. (If it isn't, you have a decision to make.)

- If you would hire the person, what would you specifically hire him to deliver? This question highlights what he does brilliantly.

- Bearing these answers in mind, describe your plans for meeting the person and making clear contracts about his or her best contribution to the team.

"How often should leaders ask themselves such questions: Every day, every week, every month?" enquired one person. "Doesn't it make people feel insecure? Shouldn't everybody have the chance to be able to 'coast' for a while?"

Great teams consist of people who embrace a certain ethic – they believe they are only as good as their next performance. "The show must go on" is the maxim, followed by: "Tomorrow's show must be even better." Certainly there must be time for 'Rest and Recovery,' otherwise results will suffer. Help is also given to individuals who experience difficult times, providing this does not become a life-style. Leaders must provide support, but also encourage people to focus on what they do brilliantly. Sometimes this means making tough calls.

You can add the complementary strengths

Take an honest reality check. Where are the gaps in your team? How can you fill these spaces? Do you have the latent talents in-house or

THE FREELANCE QUESTION

The person's name

● _____

If this person left and offered his or her services back, would I hire him or her?

YES - NO

If the answer is 'yes', I would hire this person to deliver:

● _____

● _____

● _____

Bearing these answers in mind, my plans for meeting this the person and making clear contracts about his or her best contribution to the team are:

● to _____

● to _____

● to _____

must you go scouting? Dare to take tough decisions. Don't gloss over inadequacies, because everybody will suffer. When in doubt, go out and get good people.

"Football managers have the reputation of always wanting 'two extra players," said Dave. "Despite having star defenders and forwards in our team, sometimes we failed to dominate games. Leaders were required in midfield, which is where matches are often won or lost. The club had two promising 20-year olds who could be blooded in selected matches, but not against top clubs in the Premiership. The Chairman released funds to purchase two 'old heads,' one from this country, one from abroad. Both had the ability to 'run the game' and results soon picked up. Of course, being a football manager, I still need two extra players!"

How to capitalize on your assets? Tackle the exercise called *The Super Team's Strengths Inventory*. Focus on three things. First, the Present Strengths. Describe the current talents and how to employ these gifts. Second, the Potential Strengths. Describe the latent talents and how these can be nurtured. Third, the Missing Strengths. Describe the gaps and how to fill them. Be creative on this final challenge. Certainly you might recruit full-time people. On the other hand, you can hire part-timers, contractors or brilliant niche providers. They will become part of the wider virtual Super Team.

Time to reflect on this section. Try tackling the exercise called *Strengths*. Looking back over these pages, describe three specific things you can do to capitalize on your people's talents. Then move onto the next step towards building a great team.

THE SUPER TEAM'S STRENGTHS INVENTORY

PRESENT STRENGTHS - The strengths we already have in the team are people who have the ability:

- to _____
- to _____
- to _____

The specific steps we can take to capitalise on these people's strengths are:

- to _____
- to _____
- to _____

POTENTIAL STRENGTHS - The potential strengths that we already have in the team are people who have the ability:

- to _____
- to _____
- to _____

The specific steps we can take to help people to develop these potential strengths are:

- to _____
- to _____
- to _____

MISSING STRENGTHS - The strengths we must add to the team are people who have the ability:

- to _____
- to _____
- to _____

The specific steps we can take to add people who have these potential strengths to the team are:

- to _____
- to _____
- to _____

STRENGTHS - ACTION PLAN

The specific things we can do to capitalise on people's talents in the team are:

- to _____

  _____

  _____

- to _____

  _____

  _____

- to _____

  _____

  _____

Step Two

CLARIFY THE TEAM'S
SPECIFIC GOALS

INTRODUCTION

Great teams are 'cause driven.' People strive to achieve a compelling goal that they believe is worthwhile. They follow their values, translate this into a clear vision and deliver visible results. They say things like: "We want to contribute to Live Aid and raise millions for Africa…We want to discover the structure of DNA…We want to break the four minute mile…We want to put a computer on every desk in the world…We want to find a vaccine for AIDS." People pull out all the stops to fulfill the motivating mission. Commitment oozes from every pore because everybody buys into the 'What.' Belief is the driving force. People then translate this into behavior and, where appropriate, deliver 'bottom-line' results.

What is your team's 'cause'? Can you create a one-line goal that appeals to both the heart and the head? Make sure that everybody knows:

a)   **the Picture of Perfection**
   b)   **the benefits of achieving the Picture of Perfection**
      c)   **their part in achieving the Picture of Perfection.**

People like to have a sense of ownership in shaping their part of the strategy. How to make this happen? Start by communicating, in broad terms, everybody's roles. While there are many ways to organize a team, here is one approach you might consider.

Great teams often have Compass Setters, Coordinators and Creators. Senior managers act as the Compass Setters. They set the direction, hire the right people and guide the team to success. Middle managers are the Coordinators who translate the strategy into action. Coaching is a key part of their role, as is providing support to their people. 'Front liners' are the Creators. Frequently working at the 'coal face,' much rests on their ability to provide customer satisfaction and create wealth.

People want to know their part in climbing the mountain. Clarity helps them to make their best contribution toward achieving the team goals. They like to know (a) what their role is and what it is not, and

(b) what they can decide about and what they can't decide about. Try tackling the exercise called *Clarifying People's Roles*. Bearing these answers in mind, decide which people to involve in clarifying the 'What'. They should also communicate the parameters of the 'How.' Super Teams work best when people feel they own their part of implementing the strategy.

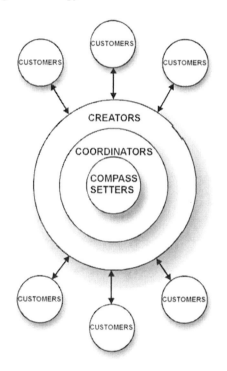

The way forward – two possible options

You now have a choice regarding the extent to which you want to involve the team in clarifying the specific goals. Option 1 is to go straight ahead to sharing the Sponsor's Picture of Perfection. You can then work with the team to shape the specific goals. (If you choose to take this route, then turn directly to page 108.) Option 2 is to do some pre-work on raising people's awareness about the challenges facing the team. Why take this second route? People will gain a wider perspective and are more likely to make better strategic decisions.

CLARIFYING PEOPLE'S ROLES

THE SENIOR TEAM

The senior team's role is:

- to _____
- to _____
- to _____
- to _____

The senior team's role is not:

- to _____
- to _____
- to _____
- to _____

The things that they can make decisions about are:

- _____
- _____
- _____
- _____

The things they cannot make decisions about are:

- _____
- _____
- _____
- _____

Bearing these answers in mind, the way they can make their best contribution to achieving these goals is:

- to _____
- to _____
- to _____
- to _____

THE MIDDLE MANAGERS

The middle managers' role is:

- to _____
- to _____
- to _____
- to _____

The middle managers' role is not:

- to _____
- to _____
- to _____
- to _____

The things that they can make decisions about are:

- _____
- _____
- _____
- _____

The things they cannot make decisions about are:

- _____
- _____
- _____
- _____

Bearing these answers in mind, the way they can make their best contribution to achieving these goals is:

- to _____
- to _____
- to _____
- to _____

THE FRONT LINERS

The front liners' role is:

- to _____
- to _____

- to _____
- to _____

The front liners' role is not:

- to _____
- to _____

- to _____
- to _____

The things that they can make decisions about are:

- _____
- _____

- _____
- _____

The things they cannot make decisions about are:

- _____
- _____

- _____
- _____

Bearing these answers in mind, the way they can make their best contribution to achieving these goals is:

- to _____
- to _____

- to _____
- to _____

You can, if appropriate, involve people in considering the big picture

For example, gather people together on an 'Away Day.' Set the scene by putting the team's task in context. After providing a short introduction, outline some themes that you want people to explore. Invite them to form groups around the particular theme they want to tackle. Here are some possible topics.

The Team's Key Challenges
People are to describe the external and internal challenges facing the team. For example, changes in the market place; improved service from competitors; developments in technology; recruiting the right people; maintaining good internal communication; etc. They are to suggest specific ways to tackle these challenges.

The Team's Present Sponsors
Invite people to list the team's present sponsors – everybody who must be satisfied if the team is to be successful. Employing their imagination, and any research data, they are to outline what each of these sponsors wants delivered. They are then to describe what the team can do to satisfy each sponsor. (Note – the exercise provides space for only one sponsor. You may want to list others on separate paper.)

The Team's Potential Sponsors
Invite people to explore future sources of business. What other potential clients might be interested in buying what the team delivers? What challenges do such potential sponsors face, both now and in the future? How could the team solve their problems and help them to achieve success? Which team members know such sponsors? How can they make contact with them and build the future business? (Again, the exercise provides space for only one potential sponsor. You may want to list others on separate paper.)

Making Clear Contracts With Sponsors: A Possible Template
This exercise invites people to consider what they must do to make clear contracts with sponsors. For example, it is important for them:

to do business with them, get solutions and achieve success. Bearing this in mind, take a look at the products and services that your team offers. Try defining what it would provide as a brilliant One Stop Shop.

Give people 30 minutes to do their chosen exercise in groups. Making flip charts to summarize their findings, they are then to present these back to the whole team. People normally produce excellent suggestions for improving the business. Let's return to the main thread of clarifying the specific goals.

THE TEAM'S KEY CHALLENGES

The key challenges we face are:

- _____
- _____
- _____
- _____
- _____
- _____

The specific things we can do to tackle these challenges successfully are:

- _____
- _____
- _____
- _____
- _____
- _____

THE TEAM'S PRESENT SPONSORS

Note. This page provides space for only one sponsor. You may wish to list others on separate paper.

The Sponsor's Name Is:

● _____

The specific things they want delivered are:

● _____

● _____

● _____

● _____

The things we can do to satisfy the sponsor are:

● _____

● _____

● _____

● _____

THE TEAM'S POTENTIAL SPONSORS

Note. This page provides space for only one sponsor. You may wish to list others on separate paper.

The potential sponsor's name is:

● _____

The challenges they face are:

● _____

● _____

● _____

The specific results they want delivered are:

● _____

● _____

● _____

The things we can do to satisfy this sponsor are:

● _____

● _____

● _____

MAKING CLEAR CONTRACTS WITH SPONSORS
- a possible template

Making clear contracts with sponsors - the specific things we should do are:

(a) to _____

　　　for example

_____

_____

_____

(b) to _____

　　　for example

_____

_____

_____

(c) to _____

    for example

_____

_____

_____

(d) to _____

    for example

_____

_____

_____

(e) to _____

    for example

_____

_____

_____

CONTROLLING THE CONTROLLABLES

CAN CONTROL - The things we can control.

● We can control _____

_____

● We can control _____

_____

● We can control _____

_____

● We can control _____

_____

● We can control _____

_____

CAN't CONTROL - The things we can't control:

● We can't control _____

_____

● We can't control _____

_____

● We can't control _____

_____

CONTROLLING THE CONTROLLABLES - Action plan

The specific things we can do to build on what we can control, and manage what we can't control, are:

● We can _____

_____

● We can _____

_____

● We can _____

_____

THE 12-MONTH
ROLLING CONTRACT

If we were on a 12-month rolling contract that had to be signed off by key sponsors every three months, the things we would do to perform great work and maintain the contract would be:

- to _____

- to _____

- to _____

- to _____

- to _____

- to _____

- to _____

- to _____

STARTING OUR OWN BUSINESS

Invite the team to imagine they are setting up a business to compete with the existing team, project or particular part of the business. They are to describe the following things:

The type of business we would run would be:

- _____

The specific customers we would target would be:

- _____

- _____

- _____

The products and services we would offer would be:

- _____

- _____

- _____

The special benefits we would offer customers would be:

- _____

- _____

- _____

The specific things we would do to be a brilliant niche provider and, in the eyes of our customers, of 'high value and hard to replace' would be:

- _____

- _____

- _____

The kind of employees we would hire - plus the number and the financial packages - would be:

- _____

- _____

- _____

The way we would organize the business - for example, the structure, location etc. - would be:

● _____

● _____

● _____

The steps we would take to get our first three customers would be:

● _____

● _____

● _____

The other things we would do to build a successful business would be:

● _____

● _____

● _____

- First, **the vision should be Positive**. For example, on an individual level, a person is more likely to succeed if they say: "I want to be healthy," rather than, "I want to stop smoking." People can reach a positive; they can't achieve a negative.

- Second, **the vision should be Precise**. Make the picture extremely detailed and specific.

- Third, **the vision should be Possible**. It should be within your gift. The Olympic Athlete may say, for example: "I aim do my personal best in the Final," rather than, "I will win." Focus on what you can control; you cannot predict the exact outcome.

- Fourth, **the vision should, in the widest sense, be Profitable**. This can be on a feeling level, as well as a financial level.

- Finally, **the vision should be made Pictorial**. If possible, produce a pictorial image of people reaching the goal.

You can ensure the vision includes the senses of seeing, hearing and feeling

Compelling visions often contain three elements that match the senses.

Seeing. The vision incorporates what you will actually be seeing when you reach the destination. For instance, the results that will be delivered; how people will be behaving; etc.

Hearing. The vision incorporates the actual words you will hear people saying.

Feeling. The vision incorporates what people will be feeling when they reach the destination.

Bearing these elements in mind, describe the actual things that will be happening when the team has reached the Picture of Perfection. For example, (a) the specific results the team will have delivered, (b) the specific words that the sponsors will be saying, or (c) the specific things that team members will be feeling.

You can theme the Picture of Perfection

You can, if you wish, sharpen the POP by identifying the key themes. For example, teams frequently produce goals that focus on the Three

Ps; Their Products, People and Profits.

- **Products** – describe the quality of the products and services that you will be delivering.
- **People** – describe what will be happening with your people. For example, the way they are working together, the morale in the team, etc.
- **Profits/Performance** – describe the specific things that will be happening in this area. For example, the delivery financial targets or other measures of performance.

You can, if appropriate, involve people in creating the team's Picture of Perfection

Continue by involving people in adding to the vision. Five steps can be taken to make this happen.

1. Put your POP on the wall or lay it out on the floor.

2. Each person is given a pad of Post-It Notes. All are then invited to write what they believe can be added to the Picture of Perfection. Invite them to make this as specific as possible. (One idea per Post-It Note.)

3. They are then to post these on the appropriate part of the Picture of Perfection.

4. After everybody has finished, gather around the completed picture. Invite people to describe what they wrote and discuss these in the group.

5. Conclude by asking for volunteers who are prepared to take away, theme and polish the agreed Picture of Perfection.

How to measure progress? After you have signed-off the final version, make the POP visual. Draw a map showing the milestones to be passed (see page 242). Put the vision in a place where people can see it every day. They are then more likely to keep working towards fulfilling the picture.

THE PICTURE OF PERFECTION
- possible themes

PRODUCTS/SERVICES: The specific things that will be happening in this area will be:

- _____
- _____
- _____

PEOPLE: The specific things that will be happening in this area will be:

- _____
- _____
- _____

PROFITABILITY/PERFORMANCE: The specific things that will be happening in this area will be:

- _____
- _____
- _____

You can use other approaches to agreeing on the team's goals

There are many models for settling on the team's targets. Some focus on the Picture of Perfection, others employ different methods. For example, here is another exercise that is tried and trusted. Gather the team together. Start by reminding people of the team's overall aims. Bearing these in mind, choose a date by which certain results must be delivered – for example, in 12 month's time. Then ask individuals to spend 5 minutes brainstorming on the topic:

The three most important goals for us to achieve in the next 12 months are:

1) to _____

2) to _____

3) to _____

Give people time to complete their brainstorming, then gather their ideas. During this part of the exercise you act as a facilitator, while somebody else records the goals on flip charts. Go around the room. Ask each person to say what they believe should be the team's top goal, which is then written on the flip chart. Continue until everybody has shared their first choice or, if the goal has already been recorded, their second choice. Go around the room again and continue until every goal is written on the flip charts.

Time to vote. Place the flip charts on the wall or lay them on the floor. Give people three voting cards (preferably ones that can be stuck on the flip charts). Each card is weighted. The first card is worth 5 votes; the second is worth 3 votes; the third is worth 1 vote. People are to vote on their top three choices. Five votes go to their top choice, three to their second, one to their third. (They can vote for goals other than those they personally suggested!)

Complete the voting. Add the scores and highlight the outstanding goals. Discuss these, integrate any overlaps and **agree on the three main goals**. Any relevant remaining items can become sub-goals. The team's aims can then be drawn as a circle of inter-dependant goals, as illustrated in the exercise *Agreeing On Common Goals*. What if the targets remain fuzzy? Ask small groups to do further work on making the goals measurable. They can then present these back to the team. As the leader, you can over-ride everything, but people normally produce what you expect. Nevertheless, your neck is on the line, so you must feel confident in signing-off the vision

You can involve people in rating the team's chances of success

Before taking the leadership role, you rated the team's chances of achieving the Picture of Perfection. Now it can be useful to involve your people in a similar discipline. Invite them to do four things. First, to list the team's goals. Second, looking at each goal in turn, to rate the present, realistic chances of delivering success. Do this on a scale 0 to 10. Third, to describe the specific things that must be done to improve the ratings. Finally, looking at the goals as a whole, they are to rate the team's chances of delivering the Picture of Perfection. Make sure the overall odds are at least 7/10.

What if some ratings fall below this score? You have several options.

- Make sure the majority of goals rate more than 7/10. Teams can still thrive if, for example, they have two goals that each rate 8/10, while one rates 6/10.

- Meet your key sponsor to manage their expectations. (Don't over promise and under deliver.) Reassure the sponsor by stressing you are committed to doing everything possible to achieve success. Bearing the present conditions in mind, however, you must be realistic. Say that you will pull out all the stops, but ask for their views on the ratings. Do they have any suggestions about how to boost the scores?

- Conclude by making clear contracts. Make sure you agree on matching expectations concerning the picture of success. What if there is a fundamental difference? Decide whether or not to continue as the leader.

AGREEING THE TEAM'S GOALS

How to involve people in agreeing on the team's goals? Here is one approach. Remind people of the team's one-line goal.

The team's one-line goal is:

● to _____

Bearing this in mind, then choose a date by which certain results must be delivered. For example: In 12 months. Then ask people to do some individual brainstorming on the topic:

The three most important goals for us to achieve in the next _____ are:

● to _____

● to _____

● to _____

Collect everybody's ideas on flipcharts. Vote on these, add the scores and highlight the outstanding goals. Integrate any overlaps and agree on The Three Main Goals. The remaining items become sub-goals of the main goals. The Team's Goals can be drawn as a circle of inter-dependant goals. The whole team can then sign-off the goals.

THE TEAM'S GOALS

The team's one-line goal is:

● to _____

Bearing this in mind, the three most important goals for us to achieve in the next _____ are:

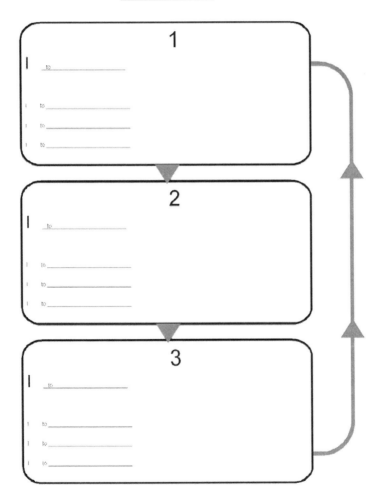

THE SUPER TEAM
- rating the chances of success

The **team's first goal** is:

● to _____

The present realistic assessment of the team's chances of achieving this goal are _____/10

The specific things that need to be done to increase the team's chances of success are:

● to _____

● to _____

● to _____

The **team's second goal** is:

● to _____

The present realistic assessment of the team's chances of achieving this goal are _____/10

The specific things that need to be done to increase the team's chances of success are:

- to _____
- to _____
- to _____

The **team's third goal** is:

- to _____

The present realistic assessment of the team's chances of achieving this goal are _____/10

The specific things that need to be done to increase the team's chances of success are:

- to _____
- to _____
- to _____

Bearing everytthing in mind, the team's chances of achieving overall success is _____/10

You can revisit the 'Why'- the team's reason for being

"Human beings will strive to achieve almost any goal," wrote Viktor Frankl, author of *Man's Search For Meaning*, "providing they see the'Why.' " People want three things from work: money, meaning and magic. Money feeds the stomach, but meaning and magic feed the spirit and the soul. They want to do valuable work and, if possible, create a meaningful legacy. People also like to embark on challenges with their eyes open. Whether they are explorers journeying to the South Pole or professionals shipping a product, they need to see both the pluses and minuses. People can then choose whether or not to buy into the whole package.

Revisit your own team's reason for being – the 'Why.' Make sure they grasp the reasons and repercussions, both for themselves and other people. Tackle the exercise called *The Super Team's Goal: Recognizing The Why*. Clarify the potential upsides and downsides for the different groups listed below. Invite people to list the pluses and minuses involved:

- for the business
- for the sponsors
- for the customers
- for potentially more 'difficult' stakeholders – for example, people whose departments may be adversely affected
- for the team
- for themselves as individuals
- for any other groups – for example, their families.

People should see the 'Why' in the pluses – it should shine like a lighted beacon. If the reasons are not self-evident, however, you will hit trouble. Take time out to discuss the minuses. "Surely there are only upsides to achieving the goals," somebody may say. There are always downsides. Sometimes this involves the personal price to be paid, other times it means upsetting people with different agendas, especially in older-style organizations. Even Art Fry, the inventor of Post-It Notes, met difficulties getting his product to market, despite the well-known entrepreneurial culture at 3M. Complete the exercise by asking your people to discuss (a) how to maximize the pluses and (b) how to manage or minimize the minuses. Bearing in mind the

You can invite people to commit themselves to achieving the goals

"Commitment is crucial, but people often just go through the motions," explained one MD. "Many 'Away Days' conclude with everybody saying they will behave differently in the future. Unfortunately their action plans often resemble New Year resolutions or wish lists. The question to ask people is: "Are you serious?" They must be committed to the commitment.

People always have options. They can make adult decisions about the route they want to follow in their personal and professional lives. Every choice has consequences, however, and there are no minus-free options. The recovering alcoholic, for example, can choose to (a) stay sober every day, (b) stay free of alcohol some days, but drink on the other days or (c) go back to drinking every day – plus lots of other options. It is no good for somebody to 'play victim,' saying: "I did not know." You want individuals who volunteer into achieving the team's goals.

State that you personally are committed to achieving the vision. Invite people to consider if they would like to go for the goals. Don't expect Billy Graham-style walks to the front, but people will probably sign-on straight away, saying things like: "Of course we are committed, there is no alternative." Providing you are satisfied, continue to the next stage, but say that you will hold follow-up meetings with each person. You will then make clear contracts about their best contribution towards delivering the Picture of Perfection.

You can, when leading a large company, communicate the purpose, principles and practice

Let's take a slight detour for a moment. What happens if you lead a large company? Certainly your senior team can set targets. People and teams throughout the business can then align their own contribution towards achieving the vision. Companies that grow dramatically, however, find it difficult to maintain a common sense of purpose.

"Five years ago we employed 100 people," explained one Managing Director. "Goal setting was easy, because it often involved survival. Today we employ over 1000 people and have become a multi-business company. Different businesses are at different stages of growth. Some must concentrate on putting in systems; others must behave like start-ups. Finance, Marketing, Human Resources, Sales, IT and other departments also have their own agendas. Sometimes, it is hard to recapture that unifying 'glue.' We want to provide a common goal, but also give people autonomy within each part of the company. Any suggestions?"

Large companies can ensure that people think Global but act Local. Imagine you are leading such a business: how can you provide a central compass but also give people a sense of ownership? Try tackling the exercise on this theme called *Purpose*. After completing it, give people a clear message about the 'rules' for making their best contribution to the business. You can communicate the company's:

Purpose   The purpose of our company is:
to _____

Principles The principles we want you to follow to achieve this purpose are, for example: to take responsibility; to be customer focused; and to deliver great results, both for the customer and our company.

Practice   The way you practice these principles will, within parameters, be up to you in your part of the business. Make sure that the way you practice them, however, supports the principles and contributes to achieving the overall purpose.

Time to reflect on this section. Try tackling the exercise called *Specific Goals*. Looking back over these pages, describe three things you can do to make sure people are focused on achieving the vision. Then move onto the next step towards building a Super Team.

THE PEAK PERFORMING COMPANY

Peak performing companies often focus on their:

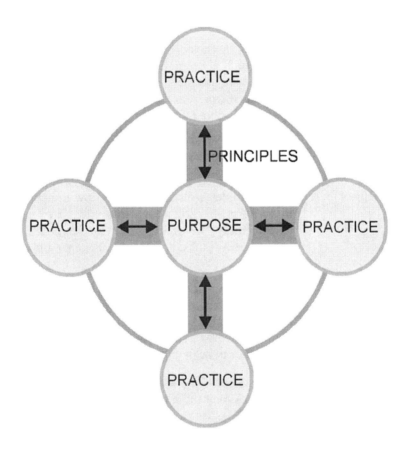

PURPOSE

PURPOSE - the purpose of our business is:

- to _____

PRINCIPLES - the principles we want to follow are:

- to _____
- to _____
- to _____
- to _____

PRACTICE - the ways that different parts of the business may want to practice these principles are:

- to _____
- to _____
- to _____
- to _____

INTRODUCTION

How can you climb the mountain? The vision is the 'What'; the strategies are the 'How.' Settle on the key things the team can do to give itself the greatest chance of success. Agree on these principles, then move onto the practice. Combining people's talents will provide the creative edge. So ask yourself: "How can we coordinate our strengths to achieve the specific goals?" Super Teams frequently adopt an approach called The Best Way. They follow four rules.

1. Get people to do what they do best.
2. Get people to work with colleagues with whom they work best.
3. Get the remaining practical tasks done in the best way.
4. Get people to make clear contracts about their best contribution to the team.

Define: "Who will do What and by When?" Let's explore how people can finalize the strategy for reaching the summit.

You can clarify the team's strategies for success

Perhaps you already have the key strategies in place, with them being implicit in your goals. If so, skip this activity. If not, invite your team to tackle the exercise called *Successful Strategies*. Bearing in mind the 'What' – the Picture of Perfection – ask people to brainstorm and then agree on:

The three key things we can do to give ourselves the greatest chance of success are:

1) to _____
2) to _____
3) to _____

Great leaders encourage people to do what works. Sounds obvious, but sometimes teams forget to follow the basics, becoming captivated by activities that are 'nice to do.' Daily disciplines are required in the Green Zone, when life is going well, just as much as in the Amber or Red Zone. "Near death experiences focus the mind," we are told. Danger acts as an alarm call and demonstrates people's ability to focus. They concentrate on the key strategies for achieving a common goal.

"September 2001's events in New York meant that many Americans, who we rely on for 50% of our trade, cancelled their reservations," said Natalie, the General Manager of a luxury hotel in London. "Faced by plunging sales, we had to regroup. I asked every manager to pull together their teams and do three things. First, to remind ourselves of our long-term vision for the hotel. Second, to give people the Successful Strategies exercise, inviting them to produce ideas on the key things we could do to deliver short, medium and longer-term results. Third, to put these suggestions forward to the senior team. We would then decide which ideas to implement.

"Colleagues rallied round; the response was phenomenal. They compiled over 50 suggestions for boosting the business. Top of the list were practical ways to attract more people from Britain. (Sounds odd, but we had neglected our home market.) We immediately produced packages for Christmas shopping, coupled with theatre nights in the West End. Other initiatives included special events for the New Year, the January Sales and the 'dark month' of February. 'Dunkirk Spirit' perhaps, but next time, I am not waiting for a crisis. Colleagues now do the exercise every six months. Everybody is encouraged to keep their eyes on the long-term vision and implement suggestions that will improve the business."

SUCCESSFUL STRATEGIES

Bearing in mind our specific goals, the three key things that we can do to give ourselves the greatest chance of success are:

1. to _____

_____

_____

2. to _____

_____

_____

3. to _____

_____

_____

SUCCESSFUL STRATEGIES
- making them happen

The first strategy is:

● to _____

The specific things we must do to implement this strategy are:

● _____

● _____

● _____

● _____

● _____

Person D's strengths

- he/she can _____

- he/she can _____

Person E's strengths

- he/she can _____

- he/she can _____

Person F's strengths

- he/she can _____

- he/she can _____

3. The **way forward** - how we can co-ordinate our strengths to reach the specific goals:

- we can _____

- we can _____

- we can _____

- we can _____

- we can _____

- we can _____

4. The **gaps** to be filled.

Gap A is:

- _____

How we can fill it:

- we can _____

Gap B is:

- _____

How we can fill it:

- we can _____

5. The **strategy** - the steps we can take to co-ordinate our strengths, fill any gaps and reach our goals are:

- we can _____
- we can _____
- we can _____
- we can _____
- we can _____

MY 'A' CONTRIBUTION

This exercise invites you to consider where you consistently deliver 'As', 'Bs' and 'Cs'. Be honest and realistic. Bearing your 'As' in mind, then clarify what you believe would be your best contribution. Follow this by describing the benefits, both to yourself and the business.

'As' - The activities where I consistently deliver 'As' are when I:

- _____
- _____
- _____
- _____

'Bs' - The activities where I consistently deliver 'Bs' are when I:

- _____
- _____
- _____
- _____

'Cs' - The activities where I consistently deliver 'Cs' are when I:

- _____
- _____
- _____
- _____

My 'A' contribution

Bearing these answers in mind, I believe my best contribution to the team would be:

- _____
- _____
- _____
- _____

The benefits of making this contribution would be:

- _____
- _____
- _____
- _____

You can get people to make clear contracts about their best contribution

Contracting is crucial. Encourage each person to take responsibility for making his or her best contribution. People who take 'ownership' for giving their best are more likely to achieve success.

How to hold such a contracting meeting? Set a date and time for the session. Make the people feel welcome, then go through the following stages.

a) Describe the team's specific goals – the Picture of Perfection.

b) Ask if they would like to contribute to achieving these goals. If so, go onto the next stage.

c) Ask them to describe their strengths and what they see as their best contribution towards achieving the team's specific goals.

d) Ask them to clarify what they see as the pluses and minuses involved – both for themselves and the team. Agree on their best contribution – the 'What.'

e) Ask them to describe 'How' they will work to deliver the goals. (Within certain parameters, the 'How' is up to them, but it is good to know their style.) Ask what support they need to do the job. Say what you can and can't offer. Ask how they will proactively keep you informed. Ask how they will get some early successes.

f) Agree on the Dos and Don'ts for working well together.

g) Finalize the contracts. Agree on 'What' they will deliver, 'How' – within parameters – and by 'When.' Invite them to complete and send you the exercise called *My Agreed Contribution To The Team*.

MY AGREED CONTRIBUTION TO THE TEAM

My agreed contributions are to:

- **(a) to** _____

Sub goals:

- to _____
- to _____
- to _____
- **(b) to** _____

Sub goals:

- to _____
- to _____
- to _____
- **(c) to** _____

Sub goals:

- to _____
- to _____
- to _____

BENEFITS

The benefits for the team are:

- _____
- _____
- _____

SUPPORT

The support I need to reach these goals is:

- _____
- _____
- _____

MEASURES

The way we will know that I have reached these goals is:

- _____
- _____
- _____

You can ensure everybody in the team makes crystal clear contracts

Communicate the Game Plan. People must know the 'What, Why, How, Who and When.' Double check they are clear on everybody's role in achieving the Picture of Perfection. (This is obviously vital in small teams, but similar principles can be applied in a large company. People should know how each department, for example, is contributing towards the specific goals. Mutual respect is then more likely to blossom.) Read through the checklist headed Contracting: The Guidelines. Bearing these points in mind, tackle the exercise on this theme. Score your team's clarity in the following categories.

● The WHAT
How do you rate people's clarity on the real results to be achieved? Do they have a clear Picture of Perfection? Rate this on a scale 0 to 10. Describe the practical steps you can take to improve the score. Make sure their understanding is at least 9/10.

● The WHY
Do people know the team's reason for being? Rate their understanding on a scale 0 to 10. Do they know the benefits for themselves, the team and the customers? Do they know the downsides? People buy pluses, rather than minuses, so make sure there will be benefits for them in achieving the goals. What practical steps can you take to improve the score?

● The HOW
Do they know the parameters within which they can operate? Do they know the Dos and Don'ts'? Rate this on a scale 0 to 10. How can you improve the score? People like to know the 'rules.' Providing people have clear guidelines, they can operate within these to achieve their goals.

● The WHO
Does everybody know each person's role in delivering success? Rate their understanding on a scale 0 to 10. Encourage people to take responsibility for making clear contracts and committing themselves to delivering the concrete results. Give them the support they need to do the job. People are prepared to be answerable for results, but make

sure you provide them with the necessary autonomy and authority.

● The WHEN

People must know the deadlines. Do they know what must be completed by whom and by when? They will then be more likely to give each other support and ensure the team reaches its goals.

Good leaders give people the opportunity to 'play back' their perception of the agreed contracts. They understand the importance of matching pictures. Looking at your team, how high does it score in the various categories? Make sure the average is at least 8/10. Clear contracting is perhaps the key step people can take towards combining their talents and achieving the Picture of Perfection.

Time to reflect on this section. Try tackling the exercise called *Strategy*. Looking back over these pages, describe three things you can do to clarify the strategies and coordinate people's strengths. Move onto the next step towards building a Super Team.

CONTRACTING - the guidelines

Clarity is vital. People must know the 'What, Why, How, Who and When.' You may want to take them through the following steps.

- Clarify The WHAT

Start from your destination. Describe the real results you want to be achieved. Communicate your Picture of Perfection. Make sure people are aware of the crystal-clear goals.

- Clarify The WHY

Clarify the rewards. Describe the reasons for achieving the goals. Describe the pluses and minuses. Make sure people are aware of the upsides and downsides in achieving the goals.

- Clarify The HOW

Clarify the rules and the parameters. Describe your leadership style. Agree on the Dos and Don'ts for achieving the goals. Agree on the support that will be required.

- Clarify The WHO

Clarify who will do what. If possible, encourage people to clarify their best contribution. Ensure people want to commit themselves to achieving the goals.

- Clarify The WHEN

Clarify the commitments - who will do what and by when? Confirm the deadlines. Clarify how people will inform you of their progress towards the goals. Finally, invite people to play back all these steps. Ensure people have a clear picture of how everybody will contribute toward delivering the Picture of Perfection.

CONTRACTING IN THE TEAM

This exercise invites you to do two things. First, to rate to what extent you believe the people in your team are clear on the 'What, Why, How, Who and When.' Do this on a scale 0-10. Second, to describe specific things you can do to improve the ratings in each of these categories.

Clarifying the WHAT

My rating as to the extent to which my
people know the 'What' is: _____/10

The specific things I can do to improve the rating are:

- _____

- _____

- _____

Clarifying the WHY

My rating as to the extent to which my
people know the 'Why' is: _____/10

The specific things I can do to improve the rating are:

- _____

- _____

- _____

Clarifying the HOW

My rating as to the extent to which my
people know the 'How' is: _____ /10

The specific things I can do to improve the rating are:

- _____
- _____
- _____

Clarifying the WHO

My rating as to the extent to which my
people know the 'Who' is: _____ /10

The specific things I can do to improve the rating are:

- _____
- _____
- _____

Clarifying the WHEN

My rating as to the extent to which my
people know the 'When' is: _____ /10

The specific things I can do to improve the rating are:

- _____
- _____
- _____

● CONCRETE RESULTS

The leader's role is to encourage, equip and ensure that people reach the Picture of Perfection. The team member's role is to keep promises, fulfill their contracts and deliver the agreed results. They should also do whatever is necessary to ensure the whole team achieves success.

● COORDINATION

Coordination from the center is vital. Strong orchestration is often required to keep the team on track. The coordinator's role is to ensure that people continually contribute towards achieving the Picture of Perfection. (Sometimes they may also 'manage' the leader. Perhaps encouraging them to focus on the big picture, for example, rather than get bogged down in details.)

Great leaders often employ a coordinator, because it releases them to drive the strategy. Would you like such a person? "But I have not got the head-count," somebody may say. The question is, do you want to spend your days (a) leading the business, (b) coordinating the business or (c) trying to do both? If you appoint somebody to fill this role, they must share the same values and professional standards. Sometimes they must make tough decisions, so they must have credibility in people's eyes.

Communicate to people (a) the role you will play in the team, (b) the role the coordinator will play. Be proactive. Spend at least two hours a week with the coordinator to look ahead, anticipate problems and find solutions. Concentrate on how to help the whole team to succeed. Clarity is the starting point for any venture – but coordination is the bridge to producing concrete results.

You can follow the STAGE model for coordination

Leaders sometimes employ the STAGE model for addressing the various aspects of teamwork. They recognize that there at least five different kinds of coordination.

1) **Strategic** – people must keep their eyes focused on the key strategies for success.

2) **Tactical** – grand plans must be translated into tactics that are

implemented each day.

3) **Administrative** – diaries must be kept up to date, meetings scheduled and the hygiene factors managed, otherwise the team falls into chaos.

4) **Grunt Work** – somebody must get their hands dirty and do the daily tasks.

5) **Emotional** – this calls for harnessing people's emotional energy to achieve the goals.

Leaders often focus on the strategic and emotional coordination. Managing the other aspects is vital, however, if the team is to achieve success. One vital point – great organizations encourage their own people to do the Great Work, that at the top of the pyramid, and subcontract the Grunt Work – not the other way round. Try tackling the exercise on this theme called *The Stage Model: Where Do I Want To Spend My Time?* You may also want to tackle the exercise called *Great Work and Grunt Work.*

GREAT WORK
AND GRUNT WORK

GREAT WORK - the specific things we can do to encourage our people to focus on doing great work are:

- to _____

- to _____

- to _____

GRUNT WORK TO KEEP - the grunt work we may want to keep when doing great work is:

- to _____

- to _____

- to _____

GRUNT WORK TO DELEGATE - the specific things we can do to delegate or sub-contract some of the grunt work are:

- to _____

- to _____

- to _____

You can encourage people to achieve their equivalent of 'The Perfect 10'

Leaders recognize the paradox. They are ultimately judged by their people's performance, not by their own. So how to boost the chances of success? Start by picking people who will do great work – that is half the battle. Then focus on being an Energizer, Encourager and Educator. (Sometimes you must act as an Enforcer, especially in crisis situations, but staying in that mode will result in becoming a life-long cop.)

Energize people by providing a compelling goal. People like to know where they are going and why. They also like to 'walk with purpose' towards the goal. Encourage people to take ownership for developing good habits. Sounds mundane, but it is necessary. Jack Nicklaus, the golfer, for example, began each season by practicing his driving, chipping and putting. He aimed to do the right thing in the right way every day. Outstanding singers, dancers, actors, artists, engineers and companies continually focus on mastering the basics. While people can be encouraged to develop such patterns, they must want to follow the disciplines. Educate them to then add those touches of magic. Let's explore how to deliver such star performances.

Peter Vidmar won a gold medal in gymnastics at the 1984 Los Angeles Olympics. Looking back at how his event was scored in those days, he describes the steps people took to achieve the Perfect 10. Firstly, they must achieve the Olympic Standard of technical competence, which often took years of dedication. This gave them the 9.4. They could then add 0.2 by taking a *Risk*, 0.2 by demonstrating *Originality* and 0.2 by showing *Virtuosity*. Such a brilliant performance produced the Perfect 10 and, hopefully, the Olympic Gold. Peter is an inspiring speaker and some people leave his sessions fired up, saying: "We can now believe in our dreams. All we have to do is to be original, take risks and demonstrate virtuosity." They only forgot one thing. Peter's most important message is that people must first achieve the 9.4.

OLYMPIC GOLD	Olympic Standard:	9.4
	Risk:	0.2
	Originality:	0.2
	Virtuosity:	0.2

The Perfect 10:   10.0

What is your team's equivalent of the 9.4? Peak performers integrate the basics so that they become second nature. They then relax and go for Gold. How to apply these lessons in your business? Try tackling the exercise called *The Super Team's Perfect 10*. Start by focusing on great habits. Describe what everybody must do to ensure the team reaches its 9.4. How can they then add star quality? Describe what everybody must do to enable the team to reach the Perfect 10. Clarify your part in making this happen by tackling the exercise called *My Perfect 10*. Super Teams insist that everybody practices good habits. People are then more likely to win their equivalent of the Olympic Gold.

You can, if appropriate, make a team credo

"The Perfect 10 exercise was the trigger for creating our Team Credo," explained Dave, the football manager. "Grand words mean nothing, however, unless they are acted upon in the heat of battle. Bold statements can actually be harmful, because you make the mistake of 'leading with a piece of paper.' We aimed to practice what we preached.

"Gathering the players together at pre-season training, we took three steps. First, we showed videos of winning sports teams, highlighting what they did well during their performances. For example, they were disciplined, especially during crises. Second, we brainstormed the 'Dos' and 'Don'ts' regarding how everybody must behave for us to be successful. Fifteen suggestions were eventually boiled down to three. We turned these into our Team Credo. Third, people then went into groups to discuss difficult situations where it might be hard to put the principles into practice. Little did we know how soon the Credo would be tested.

"The players agreed that everybody should be professional, both on and off the field," continued Dave. "The coaches discussed this with them, exploring various scenarios where it might be difficult. We then traveled to a training camp in Spain. Thirty-six hours later, five players had flown back home. Why? Reverting to the old culture, they sat in the bar, drinking with holidaymakers till 1.00 am. Everybody was watching because, as the new management team, it was our first real

test. Decisiveness was vital. The five players were told to pack their bags and find their own way back to England. Shock reverberated through the camp, but no more drinking took place. Business people may feel that having a Credo is old hat, but our players take it seriously. We see it as a foundation for success."

Would you like to make a Team Credo? (Beware, only make one if you are prepared to follow it during stormy weather.) If the answer is 'Yes,' try tackling two exercises. Start by gathering people and agreeing on *The Team Credo*. Move onto the difficult part, translating words into action, especially when times get tough. Tackle the exercise called *The Credo Challenge*. First, write the team credo. Second, describe a potential situation where it may be hard to live the Credo. Make this as realistic as possible. Third, describe the choices you will have in this situation. (If you wish, add the possible pluses and minuses of each option.) Fourth, looking at all these options, go back to the Team Credo. Agree on how you can live the Credo in this challenging situation. People will judge you by what you do, not by what you say, especially during difficult times.

You can get some early successes

Get some early wins under your belt. The rule is: "Change the physical things to change the psychological things to change the philosophical things." Long-term development may come from shifting hearts and minds, but recognize the value of quick successes. Here are some suggestions.

● Change the physical things

Start by improving the hygiene factors for your people. Pay them properly, make the building attractive and give them the tools they need to do the job. Improve the hygiene factors for your customers. For example, an online bookstore dramatically improved sales by making their web site easier to download. The technicians who designed the original site filled it with 'bells and whistles.' Customers got impatient waiting for the pictures to appear and clicked onto another bookstore's site. See things from the customer's point of view. Make it easy for them to do business with you.

(continued on page 172)

THE SUPER TEAM'S PERFECT 10

The 9.4 - the things we must all do to ensure that the team achieves the 9.4 are:

- to _____
- to _____
- to _____
- to _____
- to _____
- to _____
- to _____

The Perfect 10 - the things we must all do to ensure that the team achieves the perfect 10 are:

- to _____
- to _____
- to _____
- to _____

MY PERFECT 10

The 9.4 - the things I must do to ensure that I achieve the 9.4 are:

- to _____
- to _____
- to _____
- to _____
- to _____
- to _____
- to _____

The Perfect 10 - the things I can do to ensure that I achieve the perfect 10 are:

- to _____
- to _____
- to _____
- to _____

THE TEAM CREDO

This exercise invites you to take three steps towards creating a Team Credo. First, gather the team together and brainstorm all the 'Dos'. Describe the specific things that people must do to produce great performances. Second, narrow these down to the top five things they believe it is important to do. Ask people to make these super specific. Third, complete the exercise by compiling the Team Credo. If you wish, you can include both Dos and Don'ts.

DO:

- _____
- _____
- _____
- _____
- _____

DON'T:

- _____
- _____
- _____
- _____
- _____

THE CREDO CHALLENGE

This exercise invites you to anticipate how to 'Live The Credo' in difficult situations. First, write the team credo. Second, describe a potential situation where it may be hard to live the Credo. Make this as realistic as possible. Third, describe the choices you will have in this situation. (If you wish, add the possible pluses and minuses of each option.) Fourth, looking at all these options, go back to the Team Credo. Agree on how you can live the Credo in this challenging situation.

The **TEAM CREDO** is:

● _____

● _____

● _____

● _____

● _____

A specific situation when it may be hard to live the credo could be:

● _____

● _____

● _____

● _____

● _____

The choices we have in this situation are:

- (a) _____
- (b) _____
- (c) _____
- (d) _____
- (e) _____

The specific things we can do to live the credo in this situation could be:

- to _____
- to _____
- to _____
- to _____
- to _____

● Change the psychological things

Create a winning feeling. Highlight success stories inside the business. Publicize recent examples of great customer service. Promote people who live the values required in the future culture. Spend time with the positive people. Support the soul players and star players. Semi-detached players must decide whether they want to opt in. Recruit new people who show the drive required to reach the team's destination.

● Change the philosophical things

Great leaders harness people's emotional energy towards achieving a compelling goal. They tap into people's aspirations – be it to gain freedom, fight for justice or produce something that improves the planet. You may not offer such a life-changing experience, but you can create an inspiring vision. Remind people of the 'Why' – the benefits, both for themselves and the 'customers.' Demonstrate how far they have traveled on the journey. Start meetings by highlighting specific steps that have been taken towards the goal in the past week. Encourage people to focus on the results. They are to link whatever they say or do to how it is helping to achieve the Picture of Perfection.

Try tackling the exercise called *Getting Some Early Successes.* Producing quick wins raises people's confidence and spurs them towards their destination.

You can take proactive steps to satisfy your sponsors

"We have been given a final warning: Get our act together or our jobs will be outsourced," proclaimed Joan, the new IT Director, when addressing her people. "We have a choice. We can choose to provide good service or look for scapegoats. Customers are seldom perfect, but blaming them won't retain our jobs. We must reach out to our customers, find out what they want and help them to succeed."

A tough message? Yes. But the IT Department she took over had become insular. Problems were eventually solved for customers, but the technicians acted in a grudging manner, often neglecting to

provide the human touch. Criticism from the key sponsors was repulsed and the staff were in denial, failing to see that their jobs were on the line. Turning around the department took six months, but only one third of the original people remained. Those who stayed recognized that providing a good service was the best way to pay their mortgage.

How can you reach out to your customers? Try tackling the exercise called *Proactively Satisfying Our Sponsors*. Describe the initiatives you can take, (a) to make contact with your sponsors, (b) to find out what they want and (c) to do your best to satisfy these sponsors. Some will be unreasonable, demanding more than you can offer. Many will be delighted, however, providing you help them to succeed.

You can keep improving the team's performance

Great teams follow their purpose. They also make sure they have the right Product, People, Principles, Practice and Performance/ Profitability. Try tackling the exercise on this theme called *The Five Ps: How We Can Improve Them*. Rate your team in the following areas, then describe the steps it can take to improve the delivery

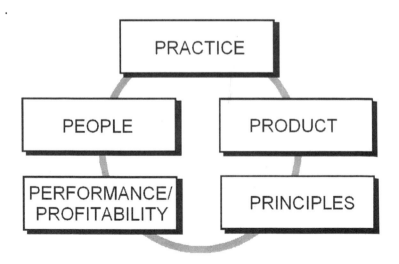

GETTING SOME
EARLY SUCCESSES

The specific things we can do to achieve some early successes are:

- to _____
- to _____
- to _____
- to _____
- to _____
- to _____
- to _____
- to _____
- to _____
- to _____
- to _____

PROACTIVELY SATISFYING OUR SPONSORS

The specific things we can do to proactively reach out and satisfy our sponsors are:

- to _____
- to _____
- to _____
- to _____
- to _____

The action plan for making this happen is:

- to _____
- to _____
- to _____
- to _____
- to _____

● PRODUCT

To what extent do you believe that your team is offering the right 'product' (or service)? Rate this on a scale 0 to 10. Is it the right one for the customers you are targeting? Is it right for the market? Is it positioned properly? Is it better than similar products offered by others? To what extent does it satisfy your sponsors or customers? (You may well have more than one product. If so, rate each of these offerings.) Describe the concrete steps you can take to improve the product.

● PEOPLE

To what extent do you believe you have the right people? Rate this on a scale 0 to 10. Are they in the right places? Do you have the right people in the senior team? Do you have a good coordinator in the team? What about people in other parts of the business – do they have the right attitude and ability? Are they Achievers? Describe the concrete steps you can take to improve the people rating.

● PRINCIPLES

To what extent do you believe the team is following the right principles? Rate this on a scale 0 to 10. Taking a helicopter view – is it focusing on the strategies most likely to achieve success? Does it deliver the right product or service to customers? Does it stay in touch with its customers? Does the team know how to build on its people's strengths? Is it committed to giving people the support they need to do the job? Describe the concrete steps the team can take to make sure it has the right principles.

● PRACTICE

To what extent do you believe the team successfully puts the principles into practice? Rate this on a scale 0 to 10. How good is it on implementation? Do people do the right thing in the right way? Do they get the right balance between consistency and creativity? Do people make their 'A' contribution to the business? Do people make the tough decisions that are sometimes necessary? Describe the concrete steps the team can take to improve the way it translates the principles into practice.

● PERFORMANCE/PROFITABILITY

How would you rate the team's present performance? (Or, where appropriate, its profitability.) Score this on a scale 0 to 10. Does the team deliver the right results? Are the sponsors and customers satisfied? While delivering today's business, is it also creating tomorrow's business? Do people get alongside potential future customers? Are they building long-term, win-win partnerships? Are they laying the foundations for future success? Describe the concrete steps the team can take to improve its performance/profitability.

You can improve the team's professional standards

How can people continually deliver high standards? The worst feedback one can receive is, "That was unprofessional." If appropriate, invite the team to tackle the exercise called *Improving Professional Standards*. They are to focus on two things. First, brainstorm the areas where they believe the team must maintain or even improve Professional Standards. For example, acting as positive models; running good meetings; following the dress code; delivering on promises; providing great service to internal and external customers, etc. Second, exploring each area in turn, describe the Dos and Don'ts regarding improving Professional Standards.

Time to reflect on this section. Tackle the exercise called *Star Performances*. Looking back over these pages, describe three concrete ways you can help your people to perform brilliantly. Then move on to the next step toward building a Super Team.

THE FIVE Ps
- how we can improve them

There are many ways to rate your performance. Here is one approach. This exercise invites you to explore to what extent you believe you have the right Product, People, Principles, Practice and Performance/ Profitability. First, rate your performance in each of these areas. Do this on a scale 0 to 10. Second, describe what you can do to improve in each area.

PRODUCT
Rate to what extent you believe you have the right product

      1   2   3   4   5   6   7   8   9   10

PEOPLE
Rate to what extent you believe you have the right people

      1   2   3   4   5   6   7   8   9   10

PRINCIPLES
Rate to what extent you believe you are following the right principles

      1   2   3   4   5   6   7   8   9   10

PRACTICE
Rate to what extent you believe the principles are being practiced properly

      1   2   3   4   5   6   7   8   9   10

PERFORMANCE/PROFITABILITY
Rate to what extent you believe you are delivering the right performance/profitability

      1   2   3   4   5   6   7   8   9   10

PRODUCT
The rating we give ourselves in this area is _____/10

The things we can do to improve in this area are:

- to _____
- to _____
- to _____

PEOPLE
The rating we give ourselves in this area is _____/10

The things we can do to improve in this area are:

- to _____
- to _____
- to _____

PRINCIPLES
The rating we give ourselves in this area is _____/10

The things we can do to improve in this area are:

- to _____
- to _____
- to _____

PRACTICE

The rating we give ourselves in this area is _____/10

The things we can do to improve in this area are:

- to _____
- to _____
- to _____

PERFORMANCE/PROFITABILITY

The rating we give ourselves in this area is _____/10

The things we can do to improve in this area are:

- to _____
- to _____
- to _____

OTHER POSSIBILITIES

The other things we can do to improve are:

- to _____
- to _____
- to _____

IMPROVING PROFESSIONAL STANDARDS

Describe the areas where you continually need to maintain - or even improve - professional standards.

The first area where we need to improve professional standards is:

- _____

The dos and don'ts in this area are:

DOs:

- do _____
- do _____
- do _____
- do _____
- do _____

DON'Ts:

- don't _____
- don't _____
- don't _____
- don't _____

STAR PERFORMANCES
- action plan

The specific things we can do to ensure that people produce star performances are:

● to _____

_____

_____

● to _____

_____

_____

● to _____

_____

_____

INTRODUCTION

Encouragement, Enterprise and **Excellence** are the steps towards creating a great environment. Start by providing people with the support they need to do the job. Spend quality time with individuals, especially the Soul Players. Why? They are often taken for granted, which can sometimes drift into neglect. Star Players require a different kind of attention. Build on their strengths, but also ensure they take responsibility for contributing towards the team's specific goals. Encouragement is the first step: but everybody must demonstrate Enterprise. You can then work together to create Excellence.

Encouragement begins on a practical level. Begin by getting the hygiene factors right, otherwise there will be problems. Pay people properly and give them the tools required to do the job. Providing they do their best, ensure people take time out to rest, re-center and refocus. Results require rest and recovery. Apart from regaining energy, people will make better decisions that benefit the business. Great teams show resilience, but all of us experience disappointments. Sometimes you may need to help individuals work through the Reactive Change Curve. Crises also arrive out of the blue, so you can educate people how to manage these successfully. Finally, encourage yourself by spending time with your own Encouragers. You will then have extra energy to pass onto the team.

How to build such a stimulating culture? The following pages provide suggestions. You may have some ideas already, however, so try tackling the exercise called *Encouragement*. Describe the specific things you can do to build a culture based on Encouragement, Enterprise and Excellence. Let's explore some other steps you can take.

THE TEAM'S ENCOURAGEMENT CONTRACT

The team's specific goals are:

- _____
- _____
- _____

The specific things we are prepared to do to reach these goals are:

- _____
- _____
- _____

The specific encouragement we would like to help us to reach these goals is:

- _____
- _____
- _____

The agreed encouragement contract is that:

- _____
- _____
- _____

THE TEAM MEMBER'S ENCOURAGEMENT CONTRACT

The specific goals I aim to achieve are:

- _____
- _____
- _____

The specific things I am prepared to do to reach these goals are:

- _____
- _____
- _____

The specific encouragement I would like to help me to reach these goals is:

- _____
- _____
- _____

The agreed encouragement contract is that:

- _____
- _____
- _____

positive people gives the 'biggest bang for the buck.' They become the 'Talismen.' They go on to produce even better work and become models for others in the team.

You can encourage people to build in time for proper rest and recovery

Climbing any mountain is arduous, so set aside periods for recovery. Apart from re-energizing the body, it is important to refresh the mind. Taking time out to re-center also enables you to make good quality decisions. Some people feel guilty about creating recovery time. Providing you have done your best, however, it is vital to recharge your batteries. Be a good model and tackle the exercise called *Results Require Proper Rest & Recovery*. Build in periods when you can regain your strength. You will then be more alert and on top of your game. Creating such 'time outs' can help to avoid losing concentration, fatigue and falling off the mountain.

Encourage people to pursue their own routes towards rest and recovery. Some may take a holiday; some may go skydiving; some may take a short sabbatical. One strategic point to remember as a leader – do not tire out your top performers by involving them in everything. Pay them for channeling their energy into what they do best. Make sure they delegate other issues to team members. Don't let your key people waste energy on details that others should be fixing. People are bound to get tired, but ensure it is on activities that capitalize on their talents.

You can encourage people to reenergize their roles

"Parts of my work are fulfilling," somebody may say, "but other parts are like wading in treacle. While I don't mind doing some donkey-work, I am not employing my strengths. Neither the team nor I are benefiting. Don't get me wrong, I want to stay in my role, but would like to re-invent it. I'd like to regain that feeling of coming to work with a spring in my step."

People sometimes find the juiciness drains out of their job. They may need a radical change, but often it is relatively easy to fix. If you wish, invite them to tackle the exercise called *Re-energizing My Role*.

Give the person a blank sheet of paper and invent them to re-craft their role afresh. They are to describe three things, (a) dos – the things they do like to do in their role, (b) don'ts – the things they don't like to do, and (c) their ideas about re-crafting their role. Reflecting on their answers, they are to cover the following themes, (a) the things they want to do in their ideal role, (b) the things they must delegate. (Boring tasks do not disappear overnight. They must show how these will be completed and give you a cast-iron guarantee.) and (c) the deliverables. They are to describe the business benefits.

"Redefining my role breathed fresh life into my job," reported one manager. "Results picked up as I spent more time on activities that helped the business. Encouraging my direct reports to attend internal meetings on my behalf, for example, gave them more visibility in the company. Several have grasped this opportunity to shine."

RESULTS REQUIRE REST & RECOVERY

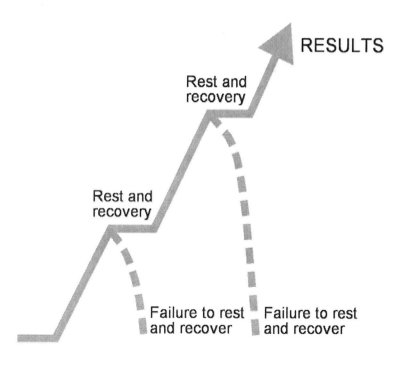

RESULTS REQUIRE PROPER REST AND RECOVERY

REST AND RECOVERY NOW - the specific things I do to rest and recover now are:

- _____
- _____
- _____
- _____
- _____

REST AND RECOVERY IN THE FUTURE - the specific things I want to do in the future to rest and recover are:

- _____
- _____
- _____
- _____
- _____

RE-ENERGIZING MY ROLE

DOs - the things I <u>do want to do</u> in the role are:

- _____
- _____
- _____
- _____
- _____
- _____
- _____
- _____

DON'Ts - the things I <u>do not want to do</u> in the role are:

- _____
- _____
- _____
- _____

RECRAFTING MY ROLE

The dos, the delegation and the deliverables

DOs - the things I want to concentrate on doing are:

- _____
- _____
- _____
- _____

DELEGATION - the things I will delegate, and ensure get done, are:

- _____
- _____
- _____

The **DELIVERABLES** - the benefits to the business will be:

- _____
- _____
- _____

You can support people during crises

How do you encourage somebody who has experienced a serious setback?' you may ask. 'Recognising a person is troubled is one thing, but I don't want to play amateur psychologist. Are there any guidelines you can follow to help them regain confidence?'

Everybody suffers disappointments in their personal or professional lives. Sometimes the problem is painful but not crippling – such as losing a customer, receiving harsh criticism or failing to win promotion. Sometimes the setback is more fundamental – such as losing a job, getting divorced or suffering a severe illness. People may then go through the Reactive Change Curve (see illustration). They travel through Shock – Denial – Paralysis – Anger – Hurt. Healing takes time. But then they climb through the stages of New Strength, New Goals, Hard Work, Success and, eventually, Self-Confidence. People are resilient. They take time to recover, but often emerge older, stronger and wiser.

THE REACTIVE CHANGE CURVE

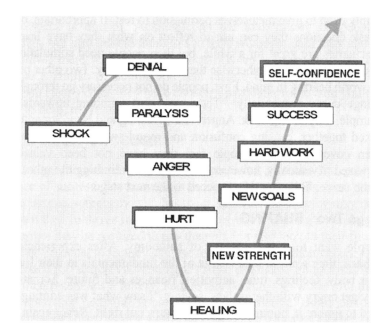

probably get hired by somebody who knows what they can deliver, rather than via a blind date. Setbacks can act as alarm calls. Sometimes the person says: "On reflection, it was the best thing that ever happened to me." Disappointments linger, but most people move on. Help them to take the steps likely to achieve long-lasting success.

You can also get encouragement

Great workers are often self-starters who love their vocation. At the same time, however, they surround themselves with people who are stimulating. Spend time with Encouragers, rather than with Stoppers. You will then have extra support and energy to pass on to the team. Try tackling the exercise called *My Self-Confidence Pot*, which was devised by Virginia Satir, a family therapist. Start by drawing an imaginary pot (see illustration.) Then go through the following steps.

Step 1: Looking at the pot, draw a line that corresponds with how high your self-confidence is today. If you have high confidence, draw it high up the pot. If your confidence is low, draw the line at a lower point. Now let's consider why it may be at this level.

Step 2: Write the names of the 'Pot Fillers.' These are the people in your life who put encouragement and energy into your pot. Similarly, you might do things yourself to put such ingredients into your pot. If you get masses of support, then 'your cup will runneth over," and you will pass-on encouragement to other people. But there may be complications, which brings us to the next part of the exercise.

Step 3: Write the names of the 'Pot Drillers.' For example: Discouragers and Energy Drainers. The more significant they are in your life, the nearer they will be to the base. Similarly, you may do things to drill holes in your own pot, such as by being overly self-critical. One other point – some people may be both Pot Fillers and Pot Drillers. For example, they may have a 'Pleasing-Hurting' pattern. Sometimes they are positive then, without warning, they lash out. Clarify the specific things they do to support or stop you.

MY SELF-CONFIDENCE POT

How high is your self-confidence? Looking at the imaginary pot, draw a line that corresponds with how high your self-confidence is today. For example, if you have high confidence, draw it high up the pot. If your confidence is low, then draw it at an appropriate level. Then write the names of the Pot Fillers, the Pot Drillers and those who do both.

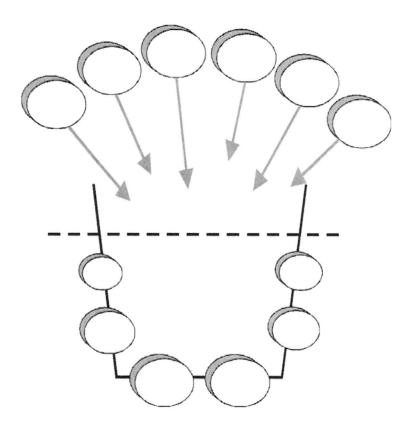

POT FILLERS

The people who put energy and encouragement into my pot are:

- _____
- _____
- _____

- _____
- _____
- _____

The things I do to put energy and encouragement into my pot are:

- _____
- _____
- _____

- _____
- _____
- _____

POT DRILLERS

The people who discourage me or take energy away are:

- _____
- _____
- _____

- _____
- _____
- _____

The things I do to discourage myself or take energy away are:

- _____
- _____
- _____
- _____
- _____
- _____

MY ACTION PLAN

The specific things I can do to put energy and encouragement into my pot are:

- to _____
- to _____
- to _____
- to _____

The specific things I can do to fill the holes in my pot are:

- to _____
- to _____
- to _____
- to _____

How to use this information? Holes in the bottom of the pot mean you will struggle to maintain the same level of confidence.

Encouragement might flow in the top, but it will drain away, sapping your energy. So what are the solutions?

Rule 1: Spend more time with people who give you energy

Energy is Life – so do the things that give you energy. Start by getting close to your Encouragers. If possible, only work with colleagues you find stimulating. Many people often find that, as they get older, they spend more time with personal and professional soul mates. Prevention is better than cure. How to increase your zest for life? Devote time to the experiences you find invigorating, such as listening to music, skiing, sailing, visiting the theatre or whatever. Pursuing these activities will put more energy into your pot.

Rule 2: Spend less time – or no time – with people who drain energy

Radical changes are difficult to make overnight but, unless the holes are filled, encouragement will simply flow out of the bottom. How to deal with Stoppers? You can do two things.

1. Stop seeing people who drain energy. Not always possible straight away, but it may be feasible in the long term. Why take this drastic step? Spending time with somebody who abuses you, for instance, is rewarding *their* behavior. The answer is to physically move away, otherwise you become a victim. But what if you want to maintain some aspects of a relationship with people who give double-messages?

2. Start making clear contracts with the people who both encourage and stop you.

   a) Reward the positive. Give clear messages about the specific things you do like them doing. Explain how you would like to build on these parts of the relationship.

   b) Give positive alternatives to the negative. Explain that: "In the future, is it possible for you to …." or "I would prefer it if you …" Present suggestions, rather than label the person as 'bad.' Don't expect people to respond immediately – everybody needs time to lick their wounds. Don't argue or fall into the blame game. What if the person refuses to respond? Then make the decision whether stay or leave.

c) Finally, when in doubt, ask yourself: "Is this activity giving me energy?" If not, switch to spending time with the people, and on the activities, that provide stimulation. Positive energy is the source of life. You will then be able to give more encouragement to the team.

Time to reflect on this section. Try tackling the exercise called *Support*. Looking back over these pages, describe three specific things you can do to ensure your people give and get encouragement. Then move onto the next step towards building a Super Team.

SUPPORT - action plan

The specific things we can do to ensure that people get and give the right kind of support are:

● to _____

_____

_____

● to _____

_____

_____

● to _____

_____

_____

Step Six

TACKLE CHALLENGES
AND FIND CREATIVE
SOLUTIONS

INTRODUCTION

Good navigators chart the route to success, but they also anticipate possible problems. Educate your team to explore any 'Sticky Moments' they may encounter on the journey. There are two reasons for doing this. First, they will find excellent solutions. Second, they will expand the team's 'Collective Radar' and ability to make decisions without looking to you for guidance. You will be released to shape tomorrow's business, rather than managing today's business. Equip people to build on early wins, because some teams 'declare victory too early.' Suddenly they lose momentum and slide down the hill. Make sure people know how to operate when in the Green Zone, Amber Zone and Red Zone. Finally, ensure everybody can manage crises. People will then be better equipped to make good decisions when it matters. Why go through such rehearsals? Super Teams in sports continually practice. Teams in organizations, however, seldom do. They play things 'off the cuff,' which can create confusion. This chapter explores how to tackle difficulties you may meet on the road to success.

You can educate people to anticipate 'Sticky Moments'

Peak performers have what is called a 'Memory of the Future.' They continually look ahead to challenges and find creative solutions. It is harder to get a whole team to develop a collective 'Radar' for managing foreseeable problems. Why is this important? When the team are under fire, two things are demonstrated - (a) people show their real character and (b) people show the team's real values.

Crises can make or break a team. Too often when the unexpected happens, however, different team members adopt radically different strategies. Such conflicts can create confusion. People worry about how the crisis was handled and the resulting 'fall-out.' How to tackle this issue? One approach is to invite the whole team to do the exercise called *Managing Potential Sticky Moments*. This involves three stages.

1) People begin by brainstorming all the possible difficult situations they may face in the future.
2) People form groups and each group chooses one particular topic to tackle.
3) People develop strategies for (a) preventing the difficulty, (b) managing the difficulty if it actually happens and (c) exploring any Positive Possibilities that might arise from the difficulty. People then present their recommendations to the whole group.

Imagine your team is tackling the exercise, what potential problems do you think they would want to explore? Here are some that other groups have considered:

- The competitors in our market place may offer a free service to customers.
- The team's budget might be cut by 50%.
- The key sponsor might be head hunted, leaving us with a new sponsor who does not believe in the project.
- The less friendly sponsors in the business may try to sabotage the project.
- The team leader, you, might leave.
- The decision we have taken not to pay a bonus this year will hit morale, productivity and next year's results.
- The tough actions we are taking to make 10% of the staff redundant will create pain.
- The knock-on effect from making people redundant can be that some of our top performers start worrying about their futures. They may be poached by rival businesses.
- The firm might be taken over.
- The on-line store we are creating might be so successful that the company's systems crash on the first day.
- The items we sell might be so popular that demand outstrips supply, leaving us with dissatisfied customers.

The last two examples highlight a key point – winning brings its own headaches. The football team that takes a 2-0 lead early in the match, for example, can feel the job is done and start to 'showboat.' Invite people to tackle the exercise called *Managing Potential Successes*. What might go well in the future? How can they build on such achievements? Good teams do such exercises regularly to cope with potential setbacks and successes. Agreeing a collective response enables them to act quickly when the 'unexpected' happens.

MANAGING POTENTIAL STICKY MOMENTS

The potential difficulty is:

- _____

_____ ____

_____

PREVENTION - The specific things we can do to prevent the potential difficulty happening are:

- to _____

_____

- to _____

_____

- to _____

_____

- to _____

_____

MANAGEMENT - The specific things we can do to manage it if it does happen are:

- to _____

_____

- to _____

_____

- to _____

_____

POSITIVE POSSIBILITIES - the positive possibilities that might emerge if, despite our efforts, it does happen are :

- _____

_____

- _____

_____

- _____

_____

MANAGING POTENTIAL SUCCESSES

The potential success is:

● _____

_____

_____

BUILDING ON THE SUCCESS

The specific things we can do to build on the success if it happens are:

● to _____

_____

● to _____

_____

● to _____

_____

● to _____

_____

You can recruit people who are good problem solvers

"We look for three qualities in people when they come to work at our Service Center," said the manager of a travel company. "They must be Positive, Professional and Problem-Solvers. Normally when people ring us they are experiencing a problem with their travel arrangements, hotel or whatever. We aim to solve their difficulty – and encourage them to book with us in the future. Everybody in the Center must therefore show these three qualities."

- **They must be Positive**. Every day we are inundated with hundreds of customer problems. Some difficulties are easy to fix, others are more complicated. Our staff must be resilient, however, because no sooner is one difficulty solved, than another appears. They must enjoy working in this kind of Center.'

- **They must be Professional.** Our people are given guidelines, rather than scripts. The two-week induction program is intensive and involves role-playing virtually every situation they will face. Expecting people to be professional is one thing, but this also calls for paying them competitively, which we do. Colleagues are more likely to give good service to customers if they are treated well within the company.'

- **They must be Problem Solvers**. We aim to solve the customer's problem while, in the process, not making the company bankrupt. Colleagues are given wide parameters within which they can find solutions. They can also occasionally step beyond these boundaries. When they deliver solutions that may create a precedent, we ask them to inform the managers so that future scenarios can be considered. Providing we make the parameters clear, however, people act as if they are running their own business. We aim to give stunning service that encourages the customer to book again with our company.'

You can educate people to manage crises successfully

How will the team react to unexpected events? You may wish to provide people with practical tools that they can use when encountering such problems. The following pages outline one model for managing crises successfully.

Step 1 – CALMNESS

Stay calm. Get an overview and see things in perspective. Things may not be as bad as they seem. On the other hand, they may be much worse! Whether you are arriving at an accident scene, counseling a troubled person or recovering from a mistake, quickly grasp the big picture. Start by identifying the key challenges to tackle. While immediate actions may need to be taken, these must also fit with the long-term goal. For example, moving an injured person may cause internal damage. Similarly, Governmental knee-jerk 'solutions' to traffic problems can store up difficulties for later years. Get all the information, then move onto the next step.

Step 2 – CLARITY

Clarify the 'Real Results' to achieve. Arriving at an accident scene, the immediate priority may be to ease the victim's pain. Longer term, the goal is to enable the victim to make a full recovery. Getting harsh customer feedback may be painful. But do you want to win the short term argument or make them a customer for life? Looking at traffic congestion, is the goal to get more cars moving more quickly? Or is it to build a sustainable transport system? Clarity about the long-term goal is crucial. Keep returning to this 'desired outcome' throughout the process to double check you are 'climbing the right mountain.' You can then move onto the next stage.

Step 3 – CREATIVITY

Crises can give birth to imaginative solutions. Looking at the real results to achieve, what are all the possible things you can do to reach these goals? Go through the following steps.

a) Consider all the 'Conventional' ways. Tried and trusted methods may already exist for tackling this problem.

b) Consider all the 'Creative' ways. For example, 'Child Line' was invented to enable young victims of abuse to ring for help. Companies created around-the-clock service by having Call Centers located on different continents.

CRISIS MANAGEMENT

Calls for focusing on:

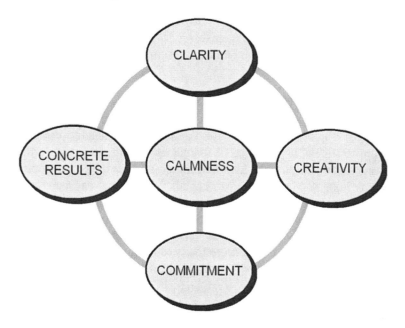

c) Consider any possible 'Combinations.' Can you combine the best parts of various options?
d) Consider the consequences of each route – the possible pluses and minuses.
e) Consider the 'attractiveness' of each route. Rate each on a scale 0 to 10.

"Do you have time for all this thinking?" somebody may ask. "Sounds like a long process." Experienced crisis managers find it quickly becomes natural and go through all the stages in a few minutes. Decide on your chosen route and move to the next step.

Step 4 – COMMITMENT
Once you have made your choice, go for it 100%. Clear contracting

is crucial. People must agree on how they will work together to achieve the concrete results. You may choose, of course, to pursue parallel strategies. Some tackle the short-term issues, while others address the long-term goals. If you adopt this route, make sure the strategies are complementary, rather than in conflict. Scientific research teams who devote themselves to finding medical cures, for example, often follow this model. Commitment to a strategy is followed by working hard.

Step 5 – CONCRETE RESULTS

Success is achieved. The road crash victim recovers, the discarded employee finds a new job, and the railway company fulfills its revamped timetable. Good crisis management calls for going further, however, and applying the key learning points. Farming catastrophes, such as Foot & Mouth Disease, contain lessons that can be used to establish healthier food practice. Disasters may sometimes be caused by an 'Act of God' – but they also provide pointers towards building a better future. Invite the team to tackle the exercise called *Crisis Management*. They are then more likely to manage unexpected events successfully.

You can rehearse what you will do in the Green Zone, Amber Zone & Red Zone

Peak performers are constantly alert, even when life is going smoothly. They do not wait for a crisis before swinging into action. Hungry for information, they scan data looking for patterns. Employing their Personal Radar, they spot the seeds of potential successes and failures long before other people. How to develop this skill? Invite your team to tackle the exercise called *The Green, Amber & Red Zones*. Ask people to describe which issues are in each zone.

CRISIS MANAGEMENT

There are many models for tackling crises. Here is one framework you can use for managing them successfully. Stay calm, but balance this with appropriate urgency. Clarity is vital: be crystal clear on the real results you want to achieve. Consider the 'conventional' options - the obvious ones - the 'creative' options and the possible 'combinations'. Clarify the consequences - the pluses and minuses - of each route. Rate each option's attractiveness. Commit yourself to an action plan, which may include pursuing parallel options, and make clear working contracts. Deliver the Concrete Results.

CRISIS - the crisis is:

● _____

1. CALMNESS - The things we can do to remain calm are:

● to _____

● to _____

● to _____

2. CLARITY - the real results we want to achieve are:

● to _____

● to _____

● to _____

the possible **combination** options are:

- **(a) to** _____

       Pluses   Minuses

- _____   ● _____
- _____   ● _____
- _____   ● _____

      Attractiveness rating _____/10

- **(b) to** _____

       Pluses   Minuses

- _____   ● _____
- _____   ● _____
- _____   ● _____

      Attractiveness rating _____/10

- **(c) to** _____

       Pluses   Minuses

- _____   ● _____
- _____   ● _____
- _____   ● _____

      Attractiveness rating _____/10

4. **COMMITMENT** - the option (or options) we want to follow are:

- to _____

- to _____

- to _____

Contracting - the contracts we will make to deliver the results are:

- to _____

- to _____

- to _____

5. **CONCRETE RESULTS** - the concrete results we will deliver - and by when - are:

- to _____

- to _____

- to _____

● **THE GREEN ZONE: When things are going well**

What might be the issues in this zone? Profits may be rising; the team members are happy; customers are giving positive feedback. Are there any warning signs? People may be pursuing 'nice to do' projects; discipline starts to slacken; customer visits become a chore. 'Football teams are never more vulnerable than when they have just taken the lead," we are told. The same rule applies in many fields. What must the team do tackle these issues in The Green Zone? For example, staying disciplined can produce even better results and minimize the possibility of getting into trouble. What other actions should it take?

● **THE AMBER ZONE: When things are going okay, but there may be warning signs**

What might be the issues in this zone? Profits may still be on track, but older products are reaching their sell-by date. Team members say they are okay, but more people are taking sick leave. Loyal customers call to say they want to stay with you, but are worried about falling service levels. What must the team do to tackle the issues in The Amber Zone?

● **THE RED ZONE: When things are not going well or when we experience real pressure**

What issues are in this zone? Results may have plummeted. Setback follows setback. Key people say they are leaving. The products you offer are out of date. Customers say: "We are looking elsewhere."

Suddenly, you face a turnaround situation. Perhaps it could have been avoided, however, if you had taken action early, especially when things were going smoothly. What must the team do to tackle the issues in The Red Zone?

PEAK PERFORMERS make the right decisions in the different zones

THE GREEN ZONE - the things that
are going well at the moment

The things that are in the GREEN ZONE at present are:

- _____
- _____
- _____
- _____
- _____
- _____

The steps we can take to build on these things are:

- _____
- _____
- _____
- _____
- _____
- _____

THE AMBER ZONE - things going

okay, but there may be warning signs

The things that are in the AMBER ZONE at present are:

- _____
- _____
- _____
- _____
- _____
- _____

The specific steps that we can take to tackle these things are:

- _____
- _____
- _____
- _____
- _____
- _____

THE RED ZONE - things not going well, or where we may be under pressure

The things that are in the RED ZONE at present are:

- _____
- _____
- _____
- _____
- _____
- _____

The specific steps that we can take to tackle these things are:

- _____
- _____
- _____
- _____
- _____
- _____

"I adapted this exercise to use with one of my sales people," explained a manager. "Adrenalin-driven by nature, he often responded well to customer crises, giving great service when in danger of losing the account. My aim was to get him to increase his alertness and sense of 'appropriate urgency.' He needed to develop the ability to prevent problems before they happened.

"Looking at each of his customers, we listed which accounts were in the Green, Amber and Red Zones. Working together, we agreed on the proactive steps he could take with each customer, even those in the Green Zone. The positive feedback was remarkable. Customers who thought they had been taken for granted reported that it was great to be wooed. Several increased their spending with us and his results went through the roof."

You can give tough news to people who need to improve their performance

"What about poor performers?" somebody may ask. Super Teams seldom contain unmotivated people, but individuals can sometimes fall short of the mark. If somebody is not reaching his or her agreed goals, you can take the following steps.

1) Clarify the Picture of Perfection

Ask yourself: "What are the specific results somebody in this role would be delivering? What are the actual words the customers would be saying about the quality of service the person was giving? What would their colleagues be saying about their professional standards?" Try describing:

My Picture of Perfection about what somebody in this role would be delivering is:

- _____
- _____
- _____

2) Clarify the person's potential

Bearing in mind this Picture of Perfection, ask yourself: "To what extent is the person delivering these results today? How would I rate them on a scale 0 to 10? What is their potential? Do they have the right attitude, ability and application? Given the right coaching, what rating do I think they can achieve?" Considering your answers, do you believe:

    a) the person has the potential to achieve the required rating?
    b) the person is more suited to another role – inside or outside the business – where they can get at least a 7/10?

Make a decision. Decide whether or not you want to help the person to master the particular role. (Morality is crucial. If you want the person to move on, it is vital that you have previously given them a clear message about improving their performance. Otherwise, the bad news comes out of the blue, leaving them with little chance to bridge the gaps.)

3) Carry out a plan to help the person achieve this Picture of Perfection

If you decide to work with the person on developing his or her performance, however, you may wish to follow this framework.

a) Set up the meeting and position it properly.
Contact the person. Explain that you want to talk about how to continue to improve his or her performance. Make it clear that it is a session about growing into a role – it is not a 'Goodbye' meeting. (Don't be afraid to say farewell to people, but there is a lot of work that can be done before such an exit.)

b) Start the meeting by welcoming the person. Explain that you want to do a 'Reality Check.' Describe what you plan to cover in the session.
Explain that you aim to explore what they do well and what they can improve. You will also share the Picture of Perfection outlining what somebody in that role must be delivering. You will then invite them to consider the possible options moving forward. Explain that, while you are aiming for a positive outcome, the session won't always be easy. Some messages may be tough to take on board. Your overall goal is, however, to get wins for both them and the business.

c) Start by asking them to do some self-evaluation. Invite them

to describe what they believe they are doing well and what they can do better in their work. **Then give your Picture of Perfection.**

Listen carefully. Ask for examples where appropriate. You need to understand the person's picture of their performance. If it is helpful, give positive but honest feedback regarding their successes. There may, however, be hard news to deliver. Communicate this by moving onto the next stage. Do not harangue them with details about their performance. Instead, talk about the desired outcome. People must have something they can aspire towards in the future. Describe your Picture of Perfection. Give them clear messages about:

The specific results somebody in this role would be delivering would be:

- _____
- _____
- _____

The actual words the customers would be saying about the kind of service you were giving them would be:

- _____
- _____
- _____

The actual words colleagues would be saying about your professional standards would be:

- _____
- _____
- _____

e) **Invite them to evaluate their own performance in relation to the Picture of Perfection. If appropriate, repeat the reality check.**

Ask them: "On a scale 0 to 10, how do you presently rate yourself in delivering such results? What do you think you must do to boost the scores?" Have a short discussion about their self-evaluation. If appropriate, share your ratings of their performance.

f) **Consider taking a 'Time Out' at this point.**

Invite the person to take time reflecting on the possible ways forward. For example: You can meet in two days to explore the options. (You don't have to adjourn for such a long time. A short break may also do the trick.) Why take a Time Out? If the tough news is unexpected, the person may need to go through the Reactive Change Curve. Don't get locked in arguments about details. Give them time to lick their wounds. The aim is for them to take ownership for deciding their future route.

But what if somebody responds negatively by saying: "You have given me no choice?" Explain that they do have options. For example, he or she:

- can ignore the reality check
- can argue about details, say you are wrong and seek another opinion
- can go through the motions of taking ideas on board, but continue as before
- can create a plan for focusing on the role and achieving an agreed Picture of Perfection
- can explore other options in the business, for example, roles where they are more likely to achieve a 10/10 for that Picture of Perfection.

g) **Let's imagine the person returns saying: "I want to try to deliver the required results."**

You can work with them to create a Coaching Contract. This should cover the following areas:

1. their specific goals
2. the steps they aim to take to play their part in achieving their goals
3. the help they would like to reach the goals
4. the specific measures that will show they have reached the goals.

You can then work together to fulfill the contract and achieve the agreed Picture of Perfection. (See the exercise on this theme.)

h) **Continue to work with the person on his or her Professional Development.**

Providing the person has the 'will,' they may be able to learn the skill. But what if they are not successful? For example, they may decide to leave or you may decide they will never get beyond 6/10 in the role. If so, help the person to move onto other things, inside or outside the business.

You can be decisive rather than let things drift

Turnarounds are painful. Professional turnarounds involve sorting out the profitability, sorting out the people and sorting out the products. Personal turnarounds involve sorting out your feelings, your future and in some cases, your finances. Problems can often be prevented, however, if individuals are decisive, rather than letting events drift. People often get angry with themselves for failing to act on the first signs of danger.

Looking at the team's progress, are there any problems on the horizon? Can you see any accidents waiting to happen? Can the team act now, rather than hope things turn out right? Try tackling the exercise on this theme. First, describe an issue where you or your team need to be decisive, rather than let things drift. Second, describe the desired results to achieve. Third, describe the specific steps you can take to shape future events, rather than hope the problems disappear.

Time to reflect on this section. Try tackling the exercise called *Solutions*. Describe how you can equip your people to find creative solutions to challenges. Then move onto the final step towards building a Super Team.

THE COACHING CONTRACT

This coaching contract is to be written by the coachee and agreed by both parties.

THE SPECIFIC GOALS

The specific results I want to achieve are:

- to _____
- to _____
- to _____
- to _____

THE COACHEE'S ROLE

The specific things I see as my responsibility in working to achieve these goals are:

- to _____
- to _____
- to _____
- to _____

THE COACH'S ROLE

The help I want from the coach to enable me to achieve these goals is:

- to _____
- to _____
- to _____
- to _____

THE MEASURES

The specific things that will be happening that will tell me I have reached my goals are:

- _____
- _____
- _____
- _____
- _____
- _____

DECISIVENESS vs DRIFT

THE DECISION MAKING AREA

The issue where I/we need to be decisive rather than letting things drift is:

● _____

_____

THE DESIRED RESULTS

The specific results I/we want to achieve on this issue are:

● _____

● _____

● _____

THE DECISIVE STEPS

The specific steps I/we can take to achieve the desired results on this issue are:

● _____

● _____

● _____

SOLUTIONS - action plan

The specific things we can do to ensure the team is superb at finding creative solutions to challenges are:

- to _____

_____

_____

- to _____

_____

_____

- to _____

_____

_____

Step Seven

ENSURE THAT THE TEAM ACHIEVES **SUCCESS**

INTRODUCTION

"When you have completed 80% of the job, there is only 80% left," is a good guideline. Poor math, perhaps, but it indicates the final hill that must be climbed. Finishing is an art: some people are fine finishers, while others have difficulty completing a book, building a house or shipping a product. Great leaders keep people's eyes on the goal. They make good decisions and assemble 'A' rated delivery teams. Encourage your people to follow good habits, work hard and reach the destination by the deadline. Satisfy your sponsors and achieve the Picture of Perfection.

Super Teams often become 'A Class Act.' How to add this star quality? Get people who have the right character, competence, consistency and creativity. Then encourage them to add that touch of class. Some teams become Pacesetters. They take the lead, maintain the lead and extend the lead. How do they make this happen? Pacesetters often create a pilot that lays the foundation for future success, rather than try to change old practices. They make the new rules for the game. What will you do after guiding the team to success? Share your knowledge with other people, then move on to the next fulfilling challenge. You may even want to build a second-generation Super Team. Let's explore these steps.

You can keep people's eyes on the team's Picture Of Perfection

Keep the vision in everybody's 'mind's eye.' People can easily get involved in the day-to-day work, so continually remind them of the destination. Create a visual 'Road Map': so they can see the milestones along the journey towards reaching the goals. Start from your destination and work backwards, describing the specific things that will be happening at each stage of the journey (see illustration.) Put this map in a place where people can see it every day.

THE PICTURE OF PERFECTION:

THE ROAD MAP AND MILESTONES

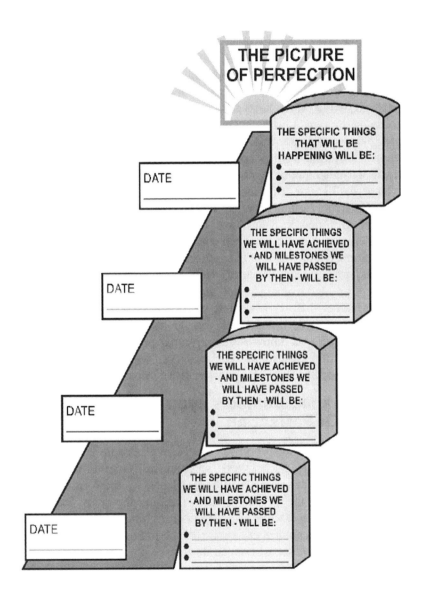

"September 2001's events led to our creating a clear vision," said Natalie, the General Manager of the luxury hotel in London. "Turnaround strategies were obviously top of the pile, but then we concentrated on the long term. During the employee workshops, we asked people to literally 'paint a picture.' Looking three years ahead, we asked them to describe and draw the hotel in 2005. For example: How did it look physically? What were guests saying about the hotel? How were the employees feeling? Combining the 80% or so ideas people had in common, we then put together a complete picture. We made copies and put them up 'back of house' throughout the building. Certainly there have been one or two changes, but these have been incorporated into the image. Whenever we hit problems, we remind ourselves of our shared vision for the future."

You can put together delivery teams that reach the destination

Great leaders are good decision makers. They also put together fine delivery teams that reach their destination by the deadline. Progress during your career often takes you through the following stages.

Stage 1: Delivery

You learn to master the job, whether this is as a sales person, programmer, chef or whatever. Growth calls for developing this skill as a Deliverer. Gaining promotion, however, often takes you onto the next stage.

Stage 2: Delivery and some decision making

You become a supervisor, team leader or 'player-manager.' Delivery still occupies much of your day, but you start making decisions that affect people in the team. Difficulties can arise, but you learn how to make clear contracts upwards, sideways and with your people. You are judged on the quality of the team's delivery and your decision-making. Gaining promotion takes you onto the next stage.

Stage 3: Decision making and building 'A-rated' delivery teams

You are now judged on two qualities. First: Your ability to make good decisions. This calls for considering the choices, the consequences and creative solutions. Choosing the best route forward reinforces the reality that there are no 'minus free' options. (Unfortunately, some so-called decision makers who reach this stage attempt to fudge the issues. They attempt to avoid making decisions, which is a decision in itself, only springing into action when hit by a disaster.) Second: Your ability to put together 'A-Rated' Delivery Teams. Destinations must be reached by a certain deadline. You cannot do all the work yourself, so you hire great people who produce the goods. Few leaders manage to master the dual skill of good decision-making and forming great delivery teams. Many revert to their old role. They go back into 'supervising' others-acting as a cop, pointing out people's mistakes. Making tough decisions and assembling fine teams can be uncomfortable. Mastering these skills, however, may mean moving onto the final stage.

Stage 4: Decision making

Strategy occupies your day. You make decisions, build models or draw maps that shape the future. Some people want to jump straight to this stage, but it helps if you have 'lived' first, having been through the fire. Like a sage who has experienced suffering, joy and peace, the wisdom is in your bones. You are then more likely to make rounded decisions that help to build a better world. So the career journey may be:

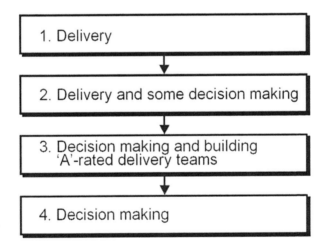

What does this mean for you as a leader? "Put together delivery teams that reach the destination by the deadline" is the maxim. Hire people with a track record of producing the goods. Contract with them on the 'What, Why, How, Who and When.' Ask them to inform you about their achievements and potential sticky moments on the journey. Keeping your eyes on the overall picture, do whatever is necessary to help the team to reach its goals.

You can ensure the team keeps working hard and delivers success

'Great groups ship," says Warren Bennis. They complete what they set out to achieve. Do you have good finishers in your team? Some individuals may appear to be self-sufficient, but check that they have everything required to ensure they deliver. What about others without such a good track record? Get alongside them. Provide encouragement, set agreed goals and support them in practicing the daily disciplines. Invite the team to tackle the exercise called *Finishing*. Ultimately, however, your head is on the block. Do whatever is necessary to ensure the team reaches its targets.

Bob Geldof inspired people to achieve a compelling goal. Stung into action after watching Michael Buerk's television report about hunger in Ethiopia, he launched Band Aid and created a Christmas single that raised £millions. He then embarked on a crusade, cutting through red tape to send food and medical supplies to Africa. That was just the start. July 13, 1985 became a day when many people rediscovered it was possible to change the world. Television showed the Live Aid concerts in Wembley and Philadelphia and the walls between nations came tumbling down. Live Aid also frightened politicians. Television showed it could reach beyond nations and restore our common humanity. Geldof reflected on his own past and was struck by the craziness of it all. He says.

One journalist, writing in Life Magazine, captured the improbability of the whole affair with a vivid image. "God had come down from heaven to find someone to undertake the task of alerting the world to the holocaust which was sweeping the continent of Africa. But this God, like the deities of old, bore the strength of fallibility and knocked at the wrong door. It was answered by Bob Geldof. 'Who the hell is he?' thought God. 'Oh, never mind, he'll do.' "

239

FINISHING

The specific things we must do to ensure we finish are:

● 1. to _____

Completed on _____

● 2. to _____

Completed on _____

● 3. to _____

Completed on _____

● 4. to _____

Completed on _____

● 5. to _____

Completed on _____

Geldof found his calling. Or rather, his calling found him. He pulled out all the stops to reach his chosen destination, rather than to decline the invitation. One year after the event, Live Aid had raised more than $100 million dollars and generated many spin-offs, such as Sports Aid. Peak performers focus on what they can do, rather about what they can't do. Do everything you can to ensure your team achieve the Picture of Perfection.

You can encourage the team to become 'A Class Act'

'They are a class act,' is a phrase used to describe a person or a team that consistently performs brilliantly – and adds that little bit extra. For example, Manchester United in the days of Best, Law and Charlton; The Three Tenors; the camera crew that shot The Blue Planet for BBC Television. Sometimes the touch of class is exemplified in a product. Designers create something that is beautiful, simple and effective. Identify a team that you believe has been 'A Class Act.' One route such groups follow is to focus on their Character, Competence, Consistency, Creativity and Class. Let's explore how your people can take these steps towards doing memorable work.

A CLASS ACT

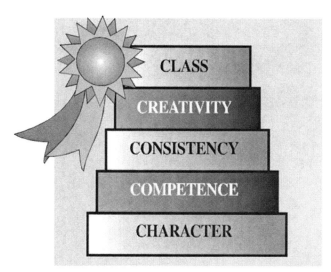

A CLASS ACT

a) Write the name of a team that you believe is, has been or has delivered, 'A Class Act.'

● _____

b) Write what you believe they did right to be 'A Class Act'.

● They _____

● They _____

● They _____

● They _____

● They _____

c) How can your team follow these paths in its own way? Describe three steps they can take to be 'A Class Act'.

● We can _____

● We can _____

● We can _____

RATING OUR TEAM
AS A CLASS ACT

How do you rate your team's performance in its chosen field? On a scale 0 to10, rate it in the following areas.

● **CHARACTER** - Rate your team on having the right attitude and character to succeed in your chosen field

   1   2   3   4   5   6   7   8   9   10

● **COMPETENCE** - Rate your team on having the skills and competence to succeed in your chosen field

   1   2   3   4   5   6   7   8   9   10

● **CONSISTENCY** - Rate your team on having the right consistency of performance to succeed in your chosen field

   1   2   3   4   5   6   7   8   9   10

● **CREATIVITY** - Rate your team on having the creativity to succeed in your chosen field

   1   2   3   4   5   6   7   8   9   10

● **CLASS** - Rate your team on having that extra touch of class that will make you outstanding in your chosen field

   1   2   3   4   5   6   7   8   9   10

CHARACTER: You can make sure the team has the right character

Looking at your people, tackle the exercise called *Rating Our Team As A Class Act*. On a scale 0 to 10: To what extent do you believe they have the right character to deliver success? Do they come to work with a spring in their step? Do they feel excited by the project? Do you have the right balance between Soul Players and Star Players? Do people support each other, especially when times get tough? Great teams often contain people who are:

● Positive

They have the right attitude and add energy to the team. They are resilient, rebound from setbacks and find solutions to challenges. They encourage other people and help their colleagues to achieve success.

● Professional

They are customer-focused and have high standards. Good at making clear contracts, they keep sponsors informed and deliver on their promises. They perform good work, establish a reputation for consistency and make a valuable contribution towards achieving the team's goals.

● Peak Performers

Building on their efforts as a team member, they also deliver outstanding work in their area of expertise, for example, as a technician, dancer, athlete, programmer, receptionist or whatever. Great teams capitalize on each person's talents. They organize the work to ensure that people do what they do best and do it often each day.

How do you rate your people? Tackle the exercise on this theme called *Positive & Professional Peak Performers*. Make sure your team has the character – and the characters – to be successful in its chosen field. Time to look at the next quality.

COMPETENCE: You can make sure the team has the right competence

Great teams possess the skills to do the job. How do you rate your team's ability? Do they have the required repertoire? On a scale 0 to 10, to what extent do they have the talent and tools needed to achieve the Picture of Perfection? Whether you orchestrate a team of technicians, surgeons, footballers or whatever, they must demonstrate professional competence. Getting the basics right provides certainty and the foundation for success.

"How do you judge whether a person has the necessary competence?" somebody may ask. The leader's job is to recognize what the person delivers. Ask yourself: "Where do they work best? What are the activities in which they come alive? When do they quickly see 'Z' – the desired Picture of Perfection? When do they have natural self-discipline? Where do they have a track record of delivering? Bearing this in mind, how can I help them to make their 'A' contribution to the team?"

Recruit people who fulfill their promises. They are 'Deliverers.' Such people demonstrate five qualities.

1. They have the DESIRE

Deliverers are passionate and full of energy. They have the drive and determination required to reach a specific goal – be it climbing a mountain, shipping a product or following a dream. Reflect back on something you have completed successfully in your life. Your desire to do it was probably at least 9/10.

2. They clarify the DESTINATION

Deliverers focus on the 'What' and have a clear Picture of Perfection. They know what they want to produce – be it a book, painting, project or whatever. Recall something you have completed successfully. Your image of the destination was probably at least 9/10. (Bear in mind that, in some cases, the end result may have been a feeling, rather than a visible product.)

POSITIVE AND PROFESSIONAL PEAK PERFORMERS
- rating our team

Great performers often demonstrate three qualities when working with both customers and colleagues. First, they are Positive. They have a positive attitude to their work and also demonstrate this in their interactions with other people. Second, they are Professional. They behave in a professional way – both towards their customers and their colleagues. Third, they are, in their areas of expertise, Peak Performers. They consistently deliver great work. This exercise invites you to rate your team and how you can improve in each of these areas.

Being POSITIVE:

	with customers	with colleagues
On a scale 0 to 10, to what extent do we demonstrate a positive attitude?	_____/10	_____/10

The specific things we can do to improve this rating are:

- We can _____
- We can _____
- We can _____
- We can _____

Being PROFESSIONAL:

	with customers	with colleagues
On a scale 0 to 10, to what extent do we demonstrate professionalism?	_____/10	_____/10

The specific things we can do to improve this rating are:

- We can _____

- We can _____

- We can _____

- We can _____

Being PEAK PERFORMERS:

	with customers	with colleagues
On a scale 0 to 10, to what extent do we deliver peak performances?	_____/10	_____/10

The specific things we can do to improve this rating are:

- We can _____

- We can _____

- We can _____

- We can _____

DEFINING MOMENTS

Getting the basics right will take you to a certain level. Then you will reach certain defining moments. Then it is vital (a) To make the right decisions and (b) to keep working to reach your chosen destination. This exercise invites your team to anticipate such critical times.

DEFINING MOMENT

The potential defining moment may be :

● when _____

DECISION MAKING

The decisions we need to take then are:

● to _____

● to _____

● to _____

DELIVERY

The specific things we must do then to deliver are:

● to _____

● to _____

● to _____

CONSISTENCY: You can make sure the team delivers consistently

How do your people rate on consistently performing fine work? Great teams score at least 8/10 in this area, which calls for developing good habits. One Olympic rowing crew reported: "The daily conditioning work became as natural as breathing or eating." Whatever the weather, they rose at 5 a.m. to run 3 miles. Winning the gold medal called for staying in shape – physically, emotionally and mentally – rather than becoming flabby. Formula 1 racing teams spend months developing wheel-changing drills to save precious seconds during a Grand Prix. They practice until the successful patterns become second nature. Invite your team to tackle the exercise on *Good Habits*.

"Daily disciplines are essential in a hotel," said Natalie, the General Manager. "Every morning we meet at 9.00 am to preview the day. Staff must know which guests are arriving and the favorite foods, drinks and flowers to put in their rooms. Staff must also know how each guest likes to use the hotel. Some guests like to be treated formally, while others tend to be more relaxed. While our staff must always be professional, they must also know the guest's preferred way of behaving. Everybody in the hotel must ensure the guest has an enjoyable stay. Failing to inform our people would make it impossible to provide a seamless service."

Consistency is crucial. Surgical teams follow set processes when performing brain operations. They then apply their individual skills within guidelines. Theatre groups perform to an agreed script, while giving some scope for interpretation. Sports teams pursue a set game plan. Then, within this framework, players are encouraged to improvise. Similar rules apply to your team. Invite people to tackle the exercise called *Consistency and Creativity*. Focus on (a) the activities that everybody must do in a consistent way and (b) the activities where, within parameters, they can be creative. Let's explore how people can make full use of their talents.

GOOD HABITS

The good habits we must all develop in order to deliver consistent performances are:

- to _____
- to _____
- to _____
- to _____
- to _____
- to _____

The benefits of developing these good habits will be:

- to _____
- to _____
- to _____
- to _____
- to _____
- to _____

CONSISTENCY AND CREATIVITY
- empowerment within parameters

CONSISTENCY

The specific things we must all do in a consistent way are:

- _____

- _____

- _____

- _____

- _____

CREATIVITY

The specific things we can do where, within parameters, we can use our creativity are:

- _____

- _____

- _____

- _____

- _____

CREATIVITY: You can make sure the team expresses appropriate creativity

Pioneers must innovate to make breakthroughs. Customer service-givers must find imaginative solutions to seemingly impossible problems. Footballers must find new ways to break down stubborn opponents in matches. On a scale 0 to 10, rate your team on having the creativity to succeed in its chosen field. How can you encourage people to use their imagination? Certainly there are 'traditional' methods for releasing their ideas, such as brainstorming. People can then take ownership for implementing the ideas. The greatest leaps in performance, however, emerge when coaching people through 'creativity in action.' How does this work in practice?

One-to-one coaching is relatively simple. First, watch the person in action. Why? Many people talk a good game, but it is vital to see how they behave in real-life. Second, ask them to do some self-evaluation. They clarify what they did well and what they could do better next time. Third, work together to build on their strengths and tackle areas for improvement. One picture is worth a thousand words, so show the new skill, rather than tell. Provide them with tools and techniques they can add to their professional repertoire. People often find such individual coaching to be intensive but rewarding.

Super Team coaching is more complicated. Why? You are dealing with an organism. Like a potter shaping clay, you must mould the team when they are in action. First, watch the team perform together. Clarify what they do well and what they can do better. Second, bearing in mind their strengths, clarify their best strategy for success. Third, communicate the strategy to people. They must understand the strategy and be committed to making it happen. Fourth, move into 'creativity in action' – on the 'practice field' or 'in rehearsal' – while the team is performing. Start by getting the basics right – make sure everybody is playing their part in the agreed 'game plan.'

Time for the exciting stage. Help the team to develop while they are performing. How? Watch them working for a few minutes. Stop the action. Then educate them – (a) how to build on what they do well and (b) how to find solutions to challenges. Like all good coaches, show rather than tell. Provide strategies, tools, skills, techniques or other options they can add to their repertoire. Encourage people to practice the new approach. Mastery calls for them making it their own – so keep going until they feel it is integrated. Provided that you educate people skillfully, the team will move to another dimension. They may well become 'A Class Act.'

Super Teams often follow The Organic Way rather than The Oppressive Way. They build on people's strengths, rather than strapping them into a straitjacket. Often such teams 'act as one.' Reporting in his book, Flow, Mihaly Csikszentmihalyi writes:

"Surgeons say that during a difficult operation they have the sensation that the entire operating team is a single organism, moved by the same purpose; they describe it as a 'ballet' in which the individual is subordinated to the group performance, and all involved share in a feeling of harmony and power."

Great teams provide us with a glimpse of paradise. The 1970 Brazilian team won the World Cup in Mexico by combining teamwork with magnificent contributions from stars such as Pele. The Riverdance Team cast a spell over TV viewers during the interval of the Eurovision Song Contest. Superb teams show what people can achieve when combining their talents. 'Going into the Zone,' they perform as if from another planet. How do they make magic? Such experiences don't just happen, concluded Mihaly. People create a sense of flow when:

1) they tackle a task which they have a chance of completing
2) they concentrate on what they are doing
3) they have clear goals
4) they get immediate feedback
5) they experience a deep and effortless involvement that removes the frustrations of everyday life
6) they enjoy a sense of control over their actions
7) they find their concern for self disappears, but paradoxically their sense of self emerges stronger
8) they find the experience is so enjoyable that their sense of time disappears.

Good educators help people to flow, focus, finish and, as a by-product, find fulfillment. "Sounds idealistic," somebody may say. "How do you make it happen in practice?" Much depends on the arena in which you perform. The following pages provide a checklist

I used as a football manager and also when educating sports coaches. (Skip this checklist if you are not interested in soccer.) Similar principles can be followed, however, whether you work in sports, business, education, the arts or wherever. See if any of the ideas can be applied to your own field. If you wish, try tackling the exercise called *Flow, Focus and Finish.* Consider how you can take people through these steps to encourage them to be creative.

"What about fulfillment?" somebody may ask. Satisfaction is often a by-product. Providing you are doing the right thing, fulfillment comes from enjoying the journey, as well as reaching the goal. Focus on the process as much as the prize. Super Teams often find that, paradoxically, they are then more likely to achieve success.

THE FLOWING WAY

You Can Encourage Your People To:

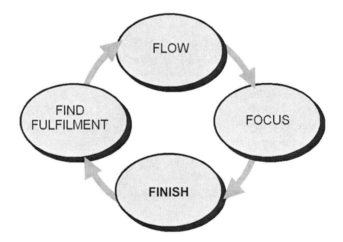

THE FLOWING WAY

FLOW

The specific things I can do to encourage the people in my team to flow are:

- to _____
- to _____
- to _____

FOCUS

The specific things I can do to encourage the people in my team to focus are:

- to _____
- to _____
- to _____

FINISH

The specific things I can do to encourage the people in my team to finish are:

- to _____
- to _____
- to _____

THE FOOTBALL MANAGER'S CHECK LIST

Choose a club you want to manage. Before taking the job, research their current circumstances. Identify the key sponsors and the results they want delivered. Clarify what you can and can't control. Watch the present team in action: recognize their strengths and areas for improvement. Clarify the resources required. Bearing this information in mind, rate the chance of success on a scale 0 to 10. Make sure the odds are at least 7/10.

If you decide to take the role, establish credibility with the sponsors. Agree on specific goals and make clear contracts. Show how you will get some quick wins. Agree on the support required and build your backroom team. Deliver an early success and, if appropriate, at this point get even more resources to improve the squad. Take the players through the following steps towards building a successful team.

Encourage the team to FLOW

● Recruit the right people with the right Spirit

Recruit players who are positive. Look for people who demonstrate leadership, take responsibility and show resilience. Watch to see if they encourage others, especially when under pressure. Invite ambitious players to join the club. Describe the club's goals. Explain how you want them to use their strengths to help the team. Give people the chance to 'opt into' the club and contribute towards achieving the specific goals.

● Build on people's Strengths

Welcome players to the pre-season training. Describe the goals for the season. Explain the principles you want the players to follow. For example: "Show a positive attitude, play positive football and you will get positive results." Explain how you expect the players to behave, on and off the field. Explain the reasoning behind the rules and the consequences of stepping over these limits. Describe the pre-season training schedule.

Make the training enjoyable and effective. Watch the team in action and build on what works. Clarify each player's best position – where they have the 'radar' and repertoire to produce results. The key point – watch for when the team works best, when the 'organism' comes alive. See which players combine well together. Build on these combinations and develop a fluent style of football. Capitalizing on these talents will make the difference in matches.

● Ensure that people know the **Specific Goals**

Gather the squad together to reiterate the goals for the season. Encourage the players to take responsibility for their performance. For example, to say: "I can do better," rather than blame the referee, the weather or whatever. Hold a one-to-one meeting with each player to contract on their specific goals.

● Ensure that people know the team's **Strategy**

Develop a flowing style of football. Create a playing system that harnesses people's strengths. Make sure the necessary tasks get done and everybody gets a chance to be creative. Communicate the system to people in the team. Provide them with 'empowerment within parameters.' Give clear messages about the playing areas where they must be 'conservative' and where they can be creative. Ensure everybody knows their role. Practice the system and play pre-season matches. Build on what works and find solutions to problems. Settle on the starting lineup before the season begins and have several games playing together. Develop a pre-match ritual that provides the platform for good performances. For example, a set travel schedule, meal, relaxation and warm up.

Encourage the team to FOCUS

● Educate people to produce **Star Performances**

Look ahead to the first game. Rehearse what may happen. Prepare people properly – physically, practically and psychologically. Make sure they know the game plan – the team's 'shape' and set moves. Ensure everybody knows what they must do (a) as team members and, on top of this (b) as individuals. Inspire the players to take a positive approach to football: to flow, focus and finish.

● **Anticipate difficulties and find Solutions**

Be aware of potential setbacks. For example, difficulties with traveling, poor pitches or gamesmanship by the opposition Anticipate problems that can occur during the game. For example, injuries, the referee making wrong decisions, going behind early, going ahead early, losing 1-0 with 10 minutes left, winning 1-0 with 10 minutes left. Foresee such situations and find creative solutions.

● **Ensure people know how to give each other Support**

Reiterate the mantra: "Be positive, play positive football and you will get positive results." Explain how you want people to support each other during the game, especially if things get tough. Explain how they are to behave towards the referee. For example, accept decisions and get on with the game, otherwise people will be fined. You need everybody on the field for the entire match.

Encourage the team to FINISH

● **Encourage people to work hard to achieve Success**

Prepare properly on the match day. (Most of the real work should have been done during the week.) Summarize the game plan and each person's part in making it happen. Get to the ground at the right time. Follow the regular pre-match warm up routines. Bring the players back into the dressing room. Repeat the key messages. Encourage people to relax, rehearse the first few minutes in their head, then go out and take charge of the match.

Encourage people during the game. (Providing you have recruited on-the-field leaders, there will be little need to convey instructions. They will work out what to do during the match.) If you give instructions, however, communicate in a simple, positive way. For example: "Put their defenders under pressure," rather than: "Don't back away from the ball."

Watch the game as a manager, not as a fan. Take a helicopter view and see patterns. Ask yourself: "What are we doing well? How can we do it more? What can we do better – and how? How can I put these messages in a way the players can accept?"

Clarify what you want to communicate at half time. Do two things. First, give the players time to calm down, treat injuries, etc. Second, call them to attention. Give a maximum of three key messages. If appropriate, give specific instructions to some players in one-to-one conversations. Keep the instructions to a minimum.

Win, lose or draw, choose your words carefully after the game. If you have won, congratulate the team. If you have lost, remind people that they are on a long journey. The next training day you will focus on what they did well and what they can improve. Invite the players to think about their own contribution over the weekend.

Resume training by looking ahead to the next match. Begin the session with a short debrief. Focus on: "What we did well during the game," and "What we can do better and how." Show how this week's training will build on these points. Work with the whole team and individual players on developing their skills. Concentrate on how to implement these in the next match.

Keep working hard and give 100% until the end of the season. Follow your principles, especially when times get tough. If necessary, educate the team to go back to basics and develop good habits. Do everything you can to deliver success.

Before the season ends, ask yourself: "Do I still feel fulfilled in this role? Do I want to continue next year? What could make it even more fulfilling?" If you want to continue:

Meet the Directors. Agree on the club's goals, the resources required and the measures of success. Meet the present players you want to keep and set specific goals. Bring in fresh blood. Look for hungry new players and secure them as soon as possible. Meet the players you want to move on and, if appropriate, help them to find new clubs. Take the next step towards building a superb team.

CLASS: You can educate the team to add that extra touch of class

Great performers make magic. Singers conclude the concert by giving a stirring encore. Chefs present a meal beautifully. Sports people produce outstanding moments that live in the memory. Different professionals have different ways of delivering such brilliance. Great designers, for example, create products that are simple, beautiful and effective. To what extent does your team currently add that touch of class? Rate this on a scale 0 to 10.

Would you like the team to show more star quality? If so, tackle the exercise called *The Super Team: Adding That Touch Of Class.* Consider the basic 'product' or service. How can you make what you offer stand out in its field? Consider the team's people skills. How can people show more 'class' in their interactions with customers? Consider the procedures that customers must follow to do business with your team. How can you improve the customer's journey and each 'moment of truth'? Consider the team's packaging. How can you present what you offer in a way that creates positive memories?

Super Teams continually 'up their game.' Looking back over this section, tackle the exercise called *Becoming A Class Act.* Describe the steps you can take to improve the team's Character, Competence, Consistency, Creativity and Class. Involve your people in this activity. It will provide the opportunity to focus on two factors. First, they will revisit the basics for delivering the 9.4. Second, they will add the touches of class that will gain their equivalent of the Olympic Gold. Then it is time to move onto the next step.

THE SUPER TEAM
- adding that touch of class

The specific things we can do to add that touch of class to
our work are:

- to _____

_____

- to _____

_____

- to _____

_____

- to _____

_____

- to _____

_____

- to _____

_____

BECOMING A CLASS ACT

This exercise invites you to focus on how your team can improve its performance in its chosen field.

CHARACTER

How we can continue to develop the right attitude and character needed to succeed in our chosen field:

● We can _____

● We can _____

● We can _____

COMPETENCE

How we can continue to develop the right skills and competencies required to succeed in our chosen field:

● We can _____

● We can _____

● We can _____

CONSISTENCY

How we can continue to develop the consistency required to succeed in our chosen field:

- We can _____
- We can _____
- We can _____

CREATIVITY

How we can continue to develop and apply the creativity required to succeed in our chosen field:

- We can _____
- We can _____
- We can _____

COMPETENCE

How we can continue to develop and demonstrate the 'class' required to succeed in our chosen field:

- We can _____
- We can _____
- We can _____

You can encourage the team to become Pacesetters

Pacesetters are pioneers. They create a prototype, product or positive model that works. Such people take the lead, maintain the lead and extend the lead. Sony invented the Walkman. First Direct popularized telephone banking. Air Miles launched a successful loyalty program. Tim Berners-Lee helped to put together the World Wide Web. Cicely Saunders founded the modern hospice movement in the UK. Lamar Hunt helped form the American Football League, and he named the Super Bowl. Pacesetters shape the future by making the new rules for the game. People, teams and companies often follow five steps towards making such breakthroughs. They focus on their:

Passion:	They follow their passion.
Purpose:	They translate their passion into a clear purpose.
Professionalism:	They do professional work.
Peak Performance:	They achieve peak performance.
Pacesetting:	They shape the future by creating positive models that work.

Pioneering teams are often 'cause driven' and want to leave a worthwhile legacy. What is your team's 'cause'? What will be its legacy? How can it shape the future? Try tackling the exercise on this theme. First, identify a team that you believe has been a Pacesetter. Second, describe what they did to perform leading edge work in their chosen field. Third, describe what your team can do to become – and remain – a Pacesetter. People are more likely to do great work when pursuing an exciting mission.

PACESETTERS

The pacesetting team's name

● _____

The things people did right to be a pacesetter in their chosen field:

● They _____

● They _____

● They _____

● They _____

● They _____

The things we can do to become - and remain - pacesetters are:

● We can _____

● We can _____

● We can _____

● We can _____

● We can _____

Pacesetters are street wise regarding how you create transformation. "Beware if you are hired to *change a culture*," said Paul, the turnaround expert. "Making a difference is possible, but choose the right vehicle." "Create A New Pilot," rather than try to "Change Old Practices." Develop a new kind of store, new way of satisfying customers or whatever. Do not get locked into meetings, trying to persuade people to change. Too many enthusiastic 'Talismen' get exhausted by systems that want to retain old habits. Run the Pilot on a 'green-field' site, where you have the practical and psychological support, rather than a 'brown-field' site. Go for Transformational Change, rather than Incremental Change. Then you have an 8/10 chance of success, rather than 3/10. Success provides its own arguments, so make the prototype work. People can choose whether to follow the new model or continue with old methods.

"There is nothing more dangerous than yesterday's success," is the oft-used warning. Pat Riley, the former NBA basketball coach, talked about 'The Innocent Climb.' Gifted teams often rise through the leagues by relying on individual brilliance. Playing off the cuff, however, they do not know how to replicate their performance. Faced by ever increasing demands, they fall apart. Similar patterns can be found in many fields. Today you may be in the Green Zone, but failure to improve creates sloppiness. People quickly slide into the Amber and Red Zones. Tough decisions are required, so go back to basics. Great teams are built on clarity. They have the right character, competence, consistency and creativity – plus that touch of class. Get the right balance between Soul Players and Star Players, then take whatever steps are necessary to build a second-generation Super Team. People will then have the chance to become, and remain, Pacesetters.

Time to reflect on this section. Try tackling the exercise called *Success*. Looking back over these pages, describe how you can ensure that your people achieve the Picture of Perfection. Then consider the next transition.

PACESETTERS

– they often run pilots that provide the foundations for future success

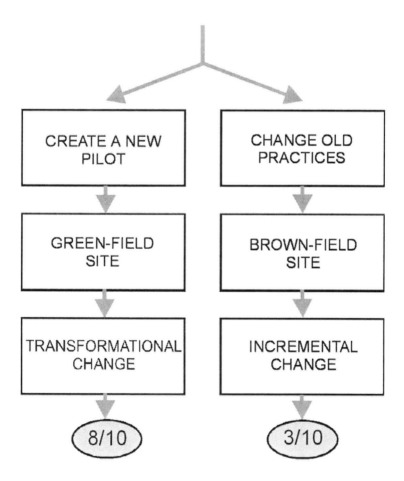

SUCCESS - action plan

The specific things we can do to ensure the team does its best to achieve success are:

- to _____

  _____

  _____

- to _____

  _____

  _____

- to _____

  _____

  _____

- to _____

  _____

  _____

CONCLUSION

Super Teams often embrace a paradox on their route towards standing on the summit. They learn to love the process as much as the prize. "Great leaders do the right things," we are told, "while managers do things right." Great teams are made up of people who do the right things in the right way, even when the leaders and managers are not around. They get the basics right – then strive to achieve the Perfect 10. Fulfillment comes from enjoying the journey, as much as reaching the goal. Success is vital, because it proves that what you do works. 'Winning' can be transitory, however, because there will always be another mountain to climb. You will get the chance to achieve another Picture of Perfection.

Looking back over the pages, can you use any of the ideas? The Eternal Truths remain constant, so your 'takeaways' are likely to be in the form of 'relearning,' rather than fresh discoveries. Tackle the final exercise called *My Action Plan*. First, describe three steps you want to take in your work. Second, describe the benefits, both for yourself and other people. Third, rate the probability of carrying out each step. Make sure the score is at least 9/10. Translate the words into action and get an early success.

Great teams often disband after reaching their destination, but some go on to scale new heights. Take time out to reflect, re-center and refocus. How can you use your gifts? How can you balance your soul work and salary work? Revisit the exercise regarding your *Vocation*. Looking into the future, what for you will be the next fulfilling challenge? What will be the right *Vehicle* for doing *Valuable Work*? Maybe you can be an individual contributor; maybe tackle an exciting project; maybe build a second-generation team. What if you choose the latter option? Start with a blank piece of paper and repeat the process. Good luck in building your next Super Team.

MY ACTION PLAN

The things I want to do in my work are:

1. to _____

The benefits of doing this will be:

_____

The probability of my doing it is: _____/10

2. to _____

The benefits of doing this will be:

_____

The probability of my doing it is: _____/10

3. to _____

The benefits of doing this will be:

_____

The probability of my doing it is: _____/10

APPENDIX 1

CANDIDATE PRE-WORK

The following pages provide exercises that you can send to a candidate before he or she comes for interview.

INTRODUCTION

Dear _____

Thank you for applying for the role. Before coming for an interview, we would like you to do some pre-work. This gives us an idea of your possible career options, your strengths and your best contribution to the business. The following pages contain exercises that we would like you to complete and return to us. Here is a little background about each of the exercises.

● My Future Work

This invites you to outline what you see as the possible routes you can pursue in the next one to two years. We obviously do not want you to break any confidences, but it is helpful if you can give an overview of your options. Obviously, there will be a temptation to say that the role for which you are applying is your preferred route. It is good to get an overview of your options, however, complete with the pluses, the minuses and the attractiveness of each route. This helps to get an overview of your thinking and can sometimes lead to other possibilities.

● My Super Strengths

What do you do brilliantly? If you were an MD, what would you hire yourself to deliver? What are the kinds of projects or activities that interest and give you energy right now? Bearing all these things in mind, what do you believe would be your best contribution to a team or business?

● My 'A' Contribution

This exercise is similar to the one on Super Strengths, but goes a little further. The future world of work has both challenging and good news. First: The Challenging News. Successful employers will only recruit, reward and retain 'A' players in each field. They will employ, for example, people who are 'A' players as leaders, managers, programmers, carpenters, receptionists and so on. They will not employ any 'B' players or 'C' players. Second: The Good News. Everybody is an 'A' player in some particular area. The key is to find where you perform at your best and show how to you can use this talent to the benefit of the employer. This exercise invites you to clarify your best contribution to a business.

● Satisfying The Key Sponsors

If you do get the opportunity to take up the role, it will be important for you to clarify your sponsor's Picture of Perfection – the results they want you to deliver. It will be also good to clarify the best way of working with them – the Dos and Don'ts. For the moment, however, we are going to ask you to use your imagination and describe three things. First: write the names of each of the potential sponsors – the people you must satisfy to thrive in the role. One will be your manager, but there may also be other key people. List each sponsor. Second: putting yourself in their shoes, what do you think will be the results they will want delivered? Write what each of the sponsors want. Third: describe what you can do to satisfy these sponsors.

● My Specific Goals

Getting some early successes will be crucial. So what will you aim to deliver in the first three months? Again, much will depend on the clear contracts you make with your sponsors – but use your imagination and describe what you will aim to deliver in the first three months.

The following pages provide the exercises. Complete these and return them. Please contact me if you would like any explanation about any of the exercises. Good luck and hope to see you at the interview.

MY FUTURE WORK

This exercise is in three parts. First, make a map of the possible roads you can take in your future work. Second, describe the pluses and minuses of each option. Third, rate how attractive each of these options is to you. Do this on a scale 0-10. Be realistic and honest when completing the exercise. This provides the opportunity for developing other possible options.

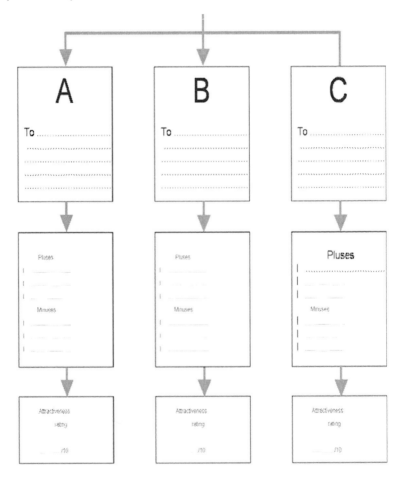

MY SUPER STRENGTHS

If you were an MD, what would you hire yourself to deliver? What are the kinds of projects or activities that interest you and give you energy right now? Bearing all these things in mind, what do you believe would be your best contribution to a team or business?

The top three things I would hire myself to deliver to a team or business are:

- To _____
- To _____
- To _____

The kinds of projects and activities that interest me right now are:

- _____
- _____
- _____

Bearing in mind my strengths and interests, I believe my best contribution to a team or business would be:

- To _____
- To _____
- To _____

MY 'A' CONTRIBUTION
TO A BUSINESS

The future world of work has both challenging and good news. First:
The Challenging News. Successful employers will only recruit, reward
and retain 'A' players in each field. They will employ, for example,
people who are 'A' players as leaders, managers, programmers,
carpenters, receptionists, etc. They will not employ any 'B' players or 'C'
players. Second: The Good News. Everybody is an 'A' player in some
particular area. The key is to find where you perform at your best and
show how to you can use this talent to the benefit of the employer.

The following exercise invites you to clarify your best contribution to an
employer.

As - the activities in which I consistently deliver As are
when I:

- _____

- _____

- _____

Bs - the activities in which I consistently deliver Bs are when I:

- _____

- _____

- _____

Cs - the activities in which I consistently deliver Cs are when I:

- _____

- _____

- _____

My 'A' contribution: I believe my best contribution to an employee would be:

- _____

- _____

- _____

SATISFYING THE KEY SPONSORS

This exercise invites you to do three things. First: write the names of each of your sponsors. Second: write what each of the sponsors wants. Third: Write what you can do to satisfy these sponsors.

The sponsor's name is:

● _____

The results they want delivered are:

● _____

● _____

● _____

The specific things I can do to satisfy this sponsor are:

● _____

● _____

● _____

The sponsor's name is:

- _____

The results they want delivered are:

- _____

- _____

- _____

The specific things I can do to satisfy this sponsor are:

- _____

- _____

- _____

The sponsor's name is:

● _____

The results they want delivered are:

● _____

● _____

● _____

The specific things I can do to satisfy this sponsor are:

● _____

● _____

● _____

SPECIFIC GOALS

The specific things I would ain to deliver in my first three months would be:

1. ● **To** _____
   Sub-goals

   ● To _____

   ● To _____

   ● To _____

1. ● **To** _____
   Sub-goals

   ● To _____

   ● To _____

   ● To _____

1. ● **To** _____
   Sub-goals

   ● To _____

   ● To _____

   ● To _____

APPENDIX 2

THE
SUPER TEAMS
WORKSHOP

The following pages provide a framework you can use when facilitating a session on building a Super Team

INTRODUCTION

How can you introduce the model to a team? The following pages outline one approach that works for facilitating a Super Teams Workshop. While some of the suggested steps may not seem to be in their 'logical' order, the flow ensures that people remain active during the session, and the framework has proved successful over the years. You can take the following steps towards running a one-day workshop on Super Teams.

Before the workshop

● **Choose to work with a leader who wants to build a Super Team**

Sounds obvious, but it is a necessary first step. Go with the energy – work with somebody who wants to introduce the ideas. You will find many leaders who want to build a Super Team.

● **Meet with the leader to do some pre-work**

Clarify the specific results they want to achieve during the workshop. The leader is the key sponsor, so ensure they will be satisfied. Clarify the key challenges facing the team. Agree with the leader whether they want these addressed. If it is a first workshop on Super Teams, however, the aim may simply be to create the right foundation. If so, you can provide people with a framework and practical tools they can use to understand:

- the principles of building a Super Team
- the practice of building a Super Team
- the practical steps they can take towards building a Super Team.

Give the leader some 'homework.' During the workshop, you will ask them to present two exercises to the team: (a) the *Picture of*

Perfection and (b) *My Leadership Style*. Invite them to complete these ahead of time. If requested, work with the leader to ensure the presentations are crystal clear.

- **Hold one-to-one meetings with each of the team.**

If possible, meet with each team member ahead of the workshop. Why? One-to-ones provide a chance to clarify the person's strengths, introduce the Super Teams model and explain the themes to be covered on the workshop. If you wish, ask the following questions.

> What do you believe should be the team's goals – The Picture of Perfection?

> Who are the team's key sponsors? What results does each sponsor want delivered?

> What are the key challenges facing the team?

> What does the team do well? What can it do even better and how?

> What are your own strengths? What do you believe would be your best contribution to the team?

> If there was only one specific thing that people could take away from the workshop, what do you think would make the session worthwhile?

- **Prepare properly ahead of the workshop.**

Finalize the running order for the workshop. Clarify the examples you will use to illustrate the themes in Super Teams. Do use examples you believe in – be these from business, sport, the arts or wherever. Don't use examples where you do not have the background knowledge. Credibility is crucial. If you give an example, make sure you can answer any 'curved ball' questions on the topic.

Finalize the materials. Produce the workshop handouts for each participant. Create the flip charts or overheads you will use during the session. Prepare The 'Super Teams Roll-Out Pack.' This contains around 30 flip chart sheets you will lay out on the floor (see Appendix 2). Mentally rehearse the workshop. Anticipate how you will overcome any potentially difficult situations. Relax and look forward to the session.

During The Workshop

● Welcome people

Get the basics right. Ensure people are greeted properly. Provide them with coffee, tea, biscuits or whatever. Make sure all the 'hygiene factors' are taken care of successfully.

● Start the workshop

Invite the leader to kick-off the session. They can give the background to the workshop – the reasons for meeting today – and outline the goals. The leader then hands over to you.

● Establish credibility

Establish credibility in your own way. Different people have different ways of demonstrating they know their subject. Follow the style that works for you.

● Describe the goals and make clear contracts

Repeat the goals for the workshop. Make clear contracts. Explain what you see as (a) your role during the day and (b) the team's role during the day. If appropriate, do a 'round the team' introduction or ice-breaker.

● Give a brief introduction to Super Teams

Again, do this in a way that fits for you. For example, I often start by saying that Super Teams have several characteristics:

> They are made up of people who take responsibility and want to opt-in.
> They have 'similarity of spirit and diversity of strengths.'
> They have the right balance between Soul Players and Star Players – no Semi-Detached Players.
> They make clear contracts. Contracting is crucial when working together to achieve the Picture of Perfection.

Other people introduce the concepts in other ways.

● Give an activity where people clarify some of the elements that make up a Super Team

People need an opportunity to 'own' the learning. So invite them to tackle the exercise called *Super Teams*. Each person is to identify a great team, plus what it did right to perform brilliant work. People then form trios and share their findings. Bring the group back together. Ask people to name the Super Teams, plus what each team did well. Write these principles on a flip chart. Keep referring back to these themes during the workshop.

● Give further input on building a Super Team

Go through the Super Teams model. In your own words, you may want to say something like: 'There are many ways to climb a mountain. Similarly, there are many ways to build a great team. Here is one approach will be looking at today.' Talk through those parts of the model that you feel are relevant. Give real-life examples that illustrate each theme.

● Invite people to create the foundations for building their own Super Team

People can now be invited to tackle the exercises on *Spirit, Sponsors, Controlling The Controllables, Professionalism, The Super Teams Contract* and *Stunning Successes*. (Prepare flip charts for each exercise ahead of time.) Put the flip charts on the floor. Ask people to stand on the topic they want to tackle and, in this way, form small groups. (You are reinforcing the voluntary principle.) People have 20 minutes to complete the exercise, including writing up the flip chart, before returning to the whole group. Each team then makes a 5-10 minute presentation. Frequently this leads to discussion. (By now it is probably time for lunch.)

Why introduce such exercises before exploring the Picture of Perfection? People will already have a rough idea of the goals. From a learning point of view, however, it is good to encourage participants to be active, rather than passive. People must also gain a sense of ownership in creating the foundations for the team. You will soon move onto the POP.

- **Put the Super Teams Roll-Out Pack on the floor. Talk people through all the steps – the exercises they can tackle – on the road towards achieving the Picture of Perfection**

Talk people through the flip charts. Start with the *Picture of Perfection* and explain each exercise, finishing with *The Milestones On The Road To The Picture Of Perfection*. Seeing the whole framework puts everything into context. People often say things like: 'It makes sense. It is like the planning process, only made simpler. It is good to see the whole picture.' Then move onto the next step.

(Please note: Find a room where you can lay out all the flip charts on the floor or, alternatively, on the wall.)

- **Invite the leader to present the Picture of Perfection**

The leader presents the Picture of Perfection. Picking a date in the future, they describe the specific things that will be happening at that time. Normally such a presentation takes around 30 minutes. One key point – it is good if the vision has been made visual on, for example, a flip chart. People are encouraged to ask questions for information. (They will later get a chance to add to the POP.) The leader then describes how they will operate. Making the 'implicit explicit,' they share My Leadership Style. People again ask questions for information. Then it is time to give them a sense of ownership in contributing to the vision.

- **Invite people to add to the POP**

Display the Picture of Perfection. Then invite people to add their ideas to the POP. You can do this in several ways. For example:

a) **When working with a <u>large team</u> where there are natural work groups,** you can invite people to go into their work groups. Give them 45 minutes to focus on two things:

> 'The Specific Things We Would Like To See Added To The POP.' They are to create a flip chart showing the things they would like to see added to the POP.

> They are also to focus on their specific contribution towards achieving the POP.

Invite them to create and present a poster showing the achievements and milestones they aim to pass on the road to the POP. For example:

'By................we will have achieved the following things – and passed the following milestones – on the road to the POP:

- _____
- _____
- _____
- _____
- _____

The contributions from each working group can then be incorporated into the road map of the milestones to be passed on the road towards the POP.

b) **When working with a <u>small team</u> where there are individual contributors,** you can invite people to follow a similar process, but this time presenting their ideas as individual contributions.

If you have time, encourage them to make their presentations on flip charts. If you do not have a lot of time, invite them to put their ideas on Post-It Notes. Each person then comes to the front and presents each idea on the Post-It as they put it on the POP. The leader then follows-up with each person later to make clear contracts about their best contribution.

Conclude this section by saying that a small group will be asked to finalize the POP. The whole team will then sign off the final version.

● **Invite people to do relevant exercises on the Roll-Out Pack (if in doubt, invite them to tackle the exercises on the Green, Amber and Red Zone.)**

People are now asked to look through the various exercises in the 'Roll-Out Pack.' Invite groups to focus on the exercises they feel are relevant. They are to tackle these exercises and make presentations back to the whole team.

If people are uncertain which exercises to choose, you can guide them by suggesting they work on the Green, Amber and Red Zone.

(These often prove relevant.) Invite people to form three groups, each focusing on one of the zones. They are then to present flip charts showing the issues that they believe are in each zone and their suggestions for tackling these challenges.

● **Invite people to form small, ongoing working groups that will focus on specific steps along the road to the Picture of Perfection**

The workshop is a beginning, not an end. So invite people to form working groups to focus on key topics. For example, *Proactively Satisfying Sponsors, Getting Early Successes, Making Tough Calls* or whatever. They must suggest specific plans for making these things happen. People are given 30 minutes to brainstorm their initial ideas and return with a short progress report. Following the workshop, they will present their action plan within two weeks. People can then implement the suggestions and build a Super Team.

● **Invite people to clarify their 'Take Away' from the day**

Time to wrap up the workshop. One approach is to ask people to clarify *Three Things I Have Learned – Or Relearned – Today*. Give individuals a few minutes to write these down by themselves, then to briefly share them, either in pairs or in the whole group. Doing such an exercise gives people a feeling of success. Thank people for their contribution to the workshop.

● **Invite the leader to conclude the session. For example: They may want to describe the next steps toward building the Super Team.**

Keep close to the leader during the day. Make sure they are happy that things are on track. During these discussions, invite them to consider how to maintain the momentum after the workshop. For example: Getting groups to report back within two weeks, implementing suggestions and getting some early successes. Ask the leader to close the workshop. When addressing their people, it is good if they outline their specific plans for continuing to build a Super Team.

Following The Workshop

● Meet with the leader

Schedule a meeting with the leader, for example, one week after the workshop. If appropriate, meet with other key people in the team. Review the 'Take Away' from the session and look forward to each group presenting their action plans. Explore how people can maintain the momentum and get some visible successes. Consider the challenges they face on the road towards achieving the Picture of Perfection.

● If appropriate, provide on-going mentoring to help people to find creative solutions to challenges

Provide on-going support. For example: The leader may like you to offer mentoring, both for themselves and their key people. You may also be asked to facilitate further sessions. Do whatever is necessary to help people to build a Super Team.

This section has described one approach to running a workshop on Super Teams. There are, of course, many other ways. One educational aid that has proved highly effective, however, is to prepare and 'walk people through' the Super Teams Roll Out Pack. This is outlined on the following pages.

APPENDIX 3

THE
SUPER TEAMS
'ROLL-OUT PACK'

You may find it useful to prepare the following flip charts. (One flip chart per sheet/exercise.) Lay these out on the floor and talk people through the steps. They can then see the whole process from A to Z. When appropriate, people can be invited to use Post-It Notes to contribute their thoughts to each flip chart. During the workshop they can create task forces to implement the suggestions. The on-going work forms the basis for follow-up sessions and ensuring they remain a Super Team.

THE PICTURE OF PERFECTION

The date is: _____

PRODUCTS/SERVICES: The specific things that will be happening in this area will be:

- _____

- _____

- _____

PEOPLE: The specific things that will be happening in this area will be:

- _____

- _____

- _____

PROFITABILITY/PERFORMANCE: The specific things that will be happening in this area will be:

- _____

- _____

- _____

THE PICTURE OF PERFECTION

SEEING - The specific results we will have delivered - and the things that will be happening - will be:

- _____
- _____
- _____

HEARING - The specific words we will be hearing people saying will be:

- _____
- _____
- _____

FEELING - The specific things people will be feeling will be:

- _____
- _____
- _____

SPIRIT

The spirit we would like people in the team to demonstrate is

(a) to _____

They would demonstrate this, for example, by:

● _____

(b) to _____

They would demonstrate this, for example, by:

● _____

(c) to _____

They would demonstrate this, for example, by:

● _____

(d) to _____

They would demonstrate this, for example, by:

● _____

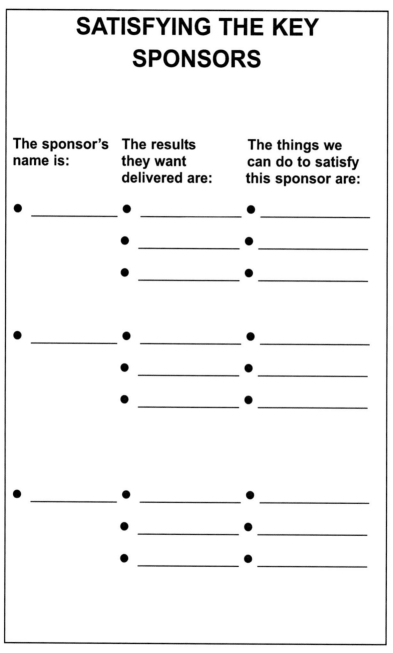

SATISFYING THE KEY SPONSORS

The sponsor's name is:	The results they want delivered are:	The things we can do to satisfy this sponsor are:
• _____	• _____	• _____
	• _____	• _____
	• _____	• _____
• _____	• _____	• _____
	• _____	• _____
	• _____	• _____
• _____	• _____	• _____
	• _____	• _____
	• _____	• _____

CONTROLLING THE CONTROLLABLES

CAN CONTROL

- We can control _____

_____ _____

_____

- We can control _____

_____ _____

_____

- We can control _____

_____ _____

_____

- We can control _____

_____ _____

_____

CAN'T CONTROL

- We can't control _____

_____ _____

_____

- We can't control _____

_____ _____

_____

- We can't control _____

_____ _____

_____

CONTROLLING THE CONTROLLABLES - action plan

The specific things we can do to build on what we can control, and manage what we can't control, are:

- We can _____

_____ _____

- We can _____

_____ _____

- We can _____

_____ _____

PROFESSIONALISM
- the Dos and Don'ts

The Dos - The specific things we must do to be super-professional in our work are:

- _____
- _____
- _____
- _____
- _____
- _____

The Don'ts - The specific things we must NOT do to be super-professional in our work are:

- _____
- _____
- _____
- _____
- _____
- _____

SUPER TEAMS CONTRACTING

The leader's responsibility is:

- to _____
- to _____
- to _____
- to _____
- to _____
- to _____

The team members' responsibility is:

- to _____
- to _____
- to _____
- to _____
- to _____
- to _____

THE TEAM'S GOALS -
recognizing the 'why'

Invite people to revisit the reason for achieving the Picture of Perfection. One way to do this is to explore the pluses and minuses involved in reaching the goals. Clarify the potential upsides and downsides for the different groups listed below. Consider these from their point of view. The pluses will embody the team's reason for achieving the Picture of Perfection. After completing the list, invite people to focus on how they can maximize the pluses and manage any minuses.

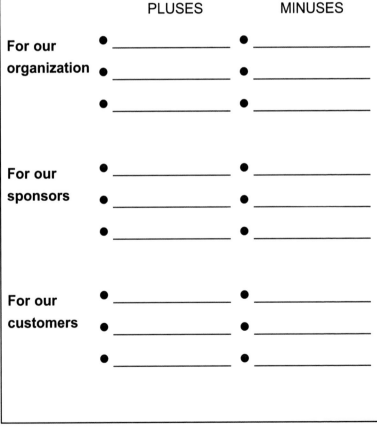

	PLUSES	MINUSES
For our organization	• _____	• _____
	• _____	• _____
	• _____	• _____
For our sponsors	• _____	• _____
	• _____	• _____
	• _____	• _____
For our customers	• _____	• _____
	• _____	• _____
	• _____	• _____

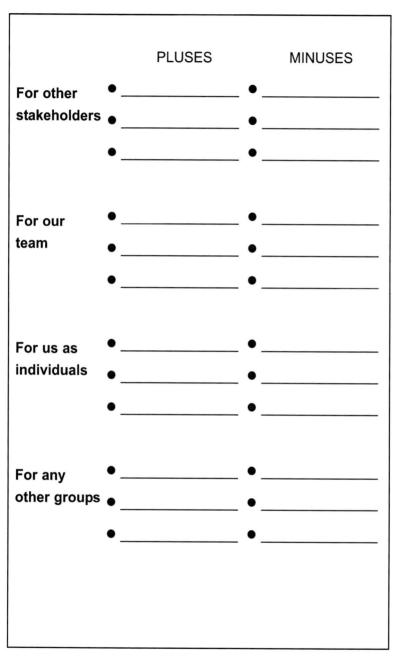

	PLUSES	MINUSES
For other stakeholders	• _____ • _____ • _____	• _____ • _____ • _____
For our team	• _____ • _____ • _____	• _____ • _____ • _____
For us as individuals	• _____ • _____ • _____	• _____ • _____ • _____
For any other groups	• _____ • _____ • _____	• _____ • _____ • _____

SUCCESSFUL STRATEGIES

Bearing in mind our specific goals, the three key things that we can do to give ourselves the greatest chance of success are:

1. to _____

_____

_____

2. to _____

_____

_____

3. to _____

_____

_____

SUCCESSFUL STRATEGIES
- making them happen

The first strategy is:

● _____

The specific things we must do to implement this strategy are:

● _____

● _____

● _____

● _____

● _____

The second strategy is:

● _____

The specific things we must do to implement this strategy
are:

● _____

● _____

● _____

● _____

● _____

The third strategy is:

● _____

The specific things we must do to implement this strategy
are:

● _____

● _____

● _____

● _____

● _____

CLARIFYING PEOPLE'S ROLES

THE SENIOR TEAM

The senior team's role is:

- to _____
- to _____
- to _____
- to _____

The senior team's role is not:

- to _____
- to _____
- to _____
- to _____

The things that they can make decisions about are:

- _____
- _____
- _____
- _____

The things they cannot make decisions about are:

- _____
- _____
- _____
- _____

Bearing these answers in mind, the way they can make their best contribution to achieving these goals is:

- to _____
- to _____
- to _____
- to _____

THE MIDDLE MANAGERS

The middle manager's role is:

- to _____
- to _____
- to _____
- to _____

The middle manager's role is not:

- to _____
- to _____
- to _____
- to _____

The things that they can make decisions about are:

- _____
- _____
- _____
- _____

The things they cannot make decisions about are:

- _____
- _____
- _____
- _____

Bearing these answers in mind, the way they can make their best contribution to achieving these goals is:

- to _____
- to _____
- to _____
- to _____

THE FRONT LINERS

The front liner's role is:

- to _____
- to _____

- to _____
- to _____

The front liner's role is not:

- to _____
- to _____

- to _____
- to _____

The things that they can make decisions about are:

- _____
- _____

- _____
- _____

The things they cannot make decisions about are:

- _____
- _____

- _____
- _____

Bearing these answers in mind, the way they can make their best contribution to achieving these goals is:

- to _____
- to _____

- to _____
- to _____

PROACTIVELY SATISFYING OUR SPONSORS

The specific things we can do to proactively go out and satisfy our sponsors are:

- to _____

_____

- to _____

_____

- to _____

_____

- to _____

_____

- to _____

_____

GETTING SOME EARLY SUCCESSES

The specific things we can do to get some early successes are:

- to _____

_____

- to _____

_____

- to _____

_____

- to _____

_____

- to _____

_____

CONSISTENCY AND CREATIVITY
- empowerment within parameters

CONSISTENCY

The specific things we must all do in a consistent way are:

- _____
- _____
- _____
- _____
- _____

CREATIVITY

The specific things we can do where, within parameters, we can use our creativity are:

- _____
- _____
- _____
- _____
- _____

THE GREEN ZONE - the things that

are going well at the moment

The things that are in the GREEN ZONE at present are:

- _____
- _____
- _____
- _____
- _____
- _____

The steps we can take to build on these things are:

- _____
- _____
- _____
- _____
- _____
- _____

THE AMBER ZONE - things going

okay, but there may be warning signs

The things that are in the AMBER ZONE at present are:

- _____
- _____
- _____
- _____
- _____
- _____

The specific steps that we can take to tackle these things are:

- _____
- _____
- _____
- _____
- _____
- _____

THE RED ZONE - things not going well, or where we may be under pressure

The things that are in the RED ZONE at present are:

- _____
- _____
- _____
- _____
- _____
- _____

The specific steps that we can take to tackle these things are:

- _____
- _____
- _____
- _____
- _____
- _____

MANAGING POTENTIAL STICKY MOMENTS

The potential difficulty is:

● _____

_____ ____

_____

PREVENTION - The specific things we can do to prevent the potential difficulty happening are:

● to _____

_____

● to _____

_____

● to _____

_____

● to _____

_____

MANAGEMENT - The specific things we can do to manage it if it does happen are:

- to _____

_____

- to _____

_____

- to _____

_____

POSITIVE POSSIBILITIES - the positive possibilities that might emerge if, despite our efforts, it does happen are :

- _____

_____

- _____

_____

- _____

_____

TOUGH CALLS

The difficult or tough decisions we may need to take are:

- to _____

_____

- to _____

_____

- to _____

_____

- to _____

_____

- to _____

_____

THE PICTURE OF PERFECTION:

THE ROAD MAP AND MILESTONES

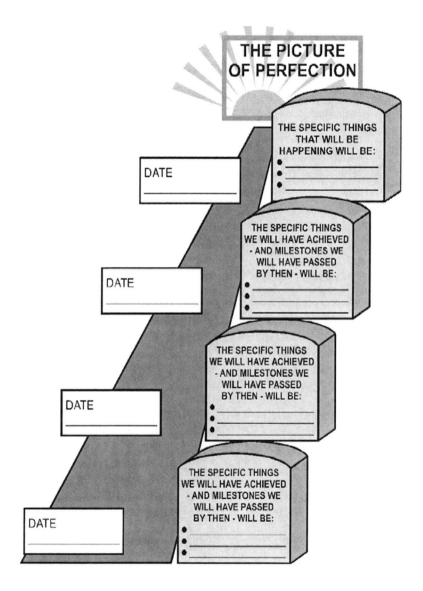

APPENDIX 4

SUPER TEAMS: SUGGESTED READING

The following books relate to building fine teams. Some titles have been mentioned in my previous books, but are included here to give an overview.

Warren Bennis and Patricia Ward Biederman, ORGANIZING GENIUS: The Secrets Of Creative Collaboration, Nicholas Brealey Publishing, 1997

"Great groups start with great people," say the authors. "Great groups think they are on a mission from God. Great groups are full of talented people who can work together. Great groups make sure the right person has the right job. Great groups ship; they deliver the goods." A fine book for anybody who wants to build a Super Team.

Bill Beswick, FOCUSED FOR SOCCER: Developing A Winning Mental Approach, Human Kinetics, 2001

One of the best books on sports psychology and the lessons can be applied to any field of work. Bill provides tips and techniques that people can use to make the best use of their talents – both as individuals and contributors to teams.

Marcus Buckingham & Don Clifton, NOW DISCOVER YOUR STRENGTHS

How do you perform World Class work? Surely it is by concentrating on 'improving' your weaknesses. Not so, say the authors: it is by learning how to leverage your talents. Marcus and Don are at the forefront of The Strengths Revolution. Packed with data, tools and ideas, this book shows how people can capitalise on what they do best.

Jim Collins, GOOD TO GREAT

"Get the right people on the bus, the wrong people off the bus and the right people in the right places on the bus," says Jim Collins. Packed with research, this is prime reading for anybody who wants to build a successful organization.

Phil Jackson & Hugh Delehanty, SACRED HOOPS: Spiritual Journeys Of A Hardwood Warrior, Hyperon, 1995

Phil Jackson is a former basketball coach of the Chicago Bulls championship winning team. He has a remarkable coaching philosophy, based on a mixture of Christianity, Zen and the Native American Indians. Well worth reading for an insight into how he got millionaire stars to submerge their egos and harness their talents into building a super team.

Jerry Lynch, CREATIVE COACHING, Human Kinetics

How can you encourage people to perform at their best? Jerry shows how the 'spiritual' approach can also prove to be successful. While drawing upon real-life case studies from sport, the author demonstrates how people can follow similar principles in their personal and professional lives. Well worth reading.

Index

Please note that the items in CAPITALS are the exercises that appear throughout the book

Endorsements

'The Super Teams Book is a great companion volume to The Magic Of Work. Being both inspirational and pragmatic, it shows how people can co-ordinate their talents to achieve success. The book goes beyond theory – it provides tools that actually work. Perhaps more importantly, the approach it outlines is transferable. Within our company, for example, leaders, managers and internal consultants have implemented the ideas to build super teams across the business. Managing a constellation of soul players and star players can be challenging, but this book shows how to make it happen.'
Steve Harvey, Steve Harvey, Group Director People,
Profit & Culture, Microsoft UK Limited

'This book unravels the mysteries of building 'Super Teams'. It offers a rich 'toolbox' that equips people to tackle the demands of the 21st century and some leading companies are following the principles to astonishing effect. The Super Team's Book offers your team practical ideas and tools that they can use to achieve outstanding success.'
Sue Moore, Managing Director, Amadeus Network Ltd

'Mike's contribution at Trayport has shown that his work provides enormous benefit to small entrepreneurial companies as well as those that are large and established. Tough as well as encouraging, he really understands teams in the workplace and what he takes to create a successful culture. The Super Teams Book captures his approach and provides a wider audience with many practical tools that companies can use to achieve success.'
Alan Deller, Chairman, Trayport Ltd

'Mike Pegg brings an approach to working together that is inspired, unique and invaluable. Building a Super Team is a privilege and proves that work can be truly rewarding. I believe that many teams can embark upon the journey offered in this book. By adapting the ideas in your own way, you will provide a stimulating environment for your people. The results will be profound. Your people will benefit, you will benefit and, most of all, your business will benefit.'
Amanda Mackenzie, Director, Marketing Services, BT Retail

'Mike is able to take an area that is full of theory and make it practical and relevant for all people who achieve their goals through teams. The Super Team approach is applicable right across our business and at all levels. It has made an impact in our organization and will continue to do so in the future.'
Roy White, Director, Human Resources, Sony Consumer Europe

'Mike Pegg has a wonderful ability for making the apparently complex seem simple and Super Teams is another example of this in action. 'Similarity of Spirit' and 'Diversity of Strengths' provides a sound framework for understanding how best to develop outstanding performance in teams. However, it is in a manager explaining his or her 'Picture of Perfection', the raw honesty of their leadership style and how best to work with them, that the real progress is made.'
Paul Mitford, Head of HR, PC World

Mike Pegg

Mike has worked as a mentor for the past 35 years. He specialises in helping people to build on their strengths and also build super teams. His clients include Microsoft, Sony, PC World, Trayport and The Dorchester Hotel. Mike is a prolific author whose books are packed with inspiring yet practical tools. *The Art of Mentoring* provides a framework for enabling mentors to pass on their wisdom. *The Magic of Work* shows people how to balance their soul work and their salary work. *The Super Teams Book*, published in December 2002, shows how teams can combine their talents to achieve success.

Like most experienced mentors, Mike has worked in many different fields. Leaving school at 15, he worked in a factory for 6 years. He then did full-time voluntary work with children with learning difficulties. After running therapeutic communities for disturbed young people, he moved on to teaching family therapy. During the early 1970s, Mike began running programmes on Strengths Building. This resulted in his being invited to educate leaders in sports and business. Since the early 1990s, he has specialised in mentoring Pacesetters – people, teams and organizations that aim to stay ahead of the field.

Mike's positive but practical approach has also reached a wider audience with appearances on TV programmes such as *The Heaven and Earth Show*.

He can be reached at:

mike @strengths.info

CPSIA information can be obtained at www.ICGtesting.com
Printed in the USA
BVOW080452290911

272157BV00005B/2/P